# It's Not Your Fault

## How Healing Relationships Change Your Brain & Can Help You Overcome a Painful Past

Patricia Romano McGraw

D1359957

*Bahá'í*
PUBLISHING
Wilmette, Illinois

MORRILL MEMORIAL LIBRARY
NORWOOD, MASS. 02062

158.1
McGraw

Bahá'í Publishing, 415 Linden Avenue, Wilmette, IL 60091-2886
Copyright © 2004 by the National Spiritual Assembly of
the Bahá'ís of the United States

All rights reserved. This book, or parts thereof, may not be
reproduced in any form without permission.

Printed in the United States of America on acid-free paper ∞
07  06  05  04    1  2  3  4

**Library of Congress Cataloging-in-Publication Data**
McGraw, Patricia Romano
    It's not your fault : how healing relationships change your brain and
can help you overcome a painful past / Patricia Romano McGraw.
      p. cm.
    Includes bibliographical references (p. ) and index.
    ISBN 1-931847-12-6 (alk. paper)
      1. Mental health. 2. Happiness. 3. Self-actualization (Psychology).
4. Attachment behavior in children. 5. Stress in children. 6. Psychic trauma
in children. 7. Interpersonal relations. 8. Spiritual life. I. Title.

RA790.5.M396 2004
158.1—dc22

                            2003063636

*Cover by Robert A. Reddy*
*Book design by Suni D. Hannan*

NORWOOD, MASS. 02062

*To Mom*

# Contents

# It's
# Not
# Your
# Fault

# Introduction

SELF-HELP BOOKS FILL THE SHELVES of our bookstores. In general, all of them have at least one common message. They tell you that you have the power to change yourself. They tell you that your life is in your hands and yours alone. And they tell you that you can heal *yourself*. By implication, all of these books are saying, if you are in pain, if you are stuck and can't seem to change, it is no one's fault but your own. You are to blame. You are not thinking positively enough. You are not organizing your life properly. You are not engaging in enough affirmations and positive self-talk. You are not prayerful enough, spiritual enough, and you are not eating the right foods. Certainly, you don't exercise enough. The magazines pick up where the self-help books leave off. Your car is not sleek enough. Your clothes aren't the right color. You need to straighten your hair, curl your hair, cut, dye, and crimp your hair. You need a new wardrobe and a new career.

If none of this works, take a walk to a different section of the bookstore. Now you *really* have a problem. This is the "Mental Health" section. Listen to Prozac. Take medication. Pick the right therapist. Get psychotherapy. Join the right support group. Go to Narcotics Anonymous, Alcoholics Anonymous, Weight Watchers, or Shapes. If none of *that* works, go to a good psychiatric hospital and stay a long time. You really need help.

None of this advice is necessarily wrong, nor do I mean to trivialize the very serious issue of mental illnesses that do require psychiatric diagnosis and treatment. However, over the years, I have worked with countless wonderful, sincere, intelligent, and highly motivated people who have followed all of the prescribed pathways and still felt depressed, anxious, inadequate, unloved, and unlovable. In short, they felt terrible, and they couldn't figure out why. They had read all the books, joined all the groups, and had even taken medicine. Finally, they had tried to just pull themselves up by their own bootstraps and tough it out alone. No matter what they tried, it just didn't work. No matter how hard they worked on themselves, they still felt fundamentally flawed, broken, and to blame for that. Many of them confided to me that they believed God or the universe had somehow made them wrong from the beginning. "There is something wrong with me," they would say. Many of them told me that they felt hopeless, ready to give up. Some, in fact, had tried to harm themselves, or constantly just wished they were dead. For others, the pain was not as severe. Instead, they complained that they felt numb or "fake," only "going through the motions of life" and not really living. They complained of a deep emptiness inside and of confusion *about who they really were*. For some, the difficulties they felt inside were played out in relationships. I encountered women and men who tolerated bad, even abusive, relationships; battered women; men who could not sustain long-term relationships; adolescents who were in trouble at school or in conflict with family and friends.

Many of these people had turned to various addictions to try to ease the pain—drugs, alcohol, sex, food, and other substances or activities—all to numb the pain. Others acted out their pain in outbursts of rage that harmed themselves or other people. The cost of acting out rage is very high; it often results in trouble with the law, ruined relationships, and lost opportunities.

When I was a new therapist more than twenty-five years ago, I remember telling folks like these to just get over their symptoms. I would tell them to quit thinking they were no good and to remember they were as good as everyone else. I would tell them to quit hurting themselves, to be kind and nice to themselves. I would tell them to quit getting involved in bad relationships and to quit their addictive and self-destructive behaviors. I would, in fact, tell them what all of today's self-help books tell them. And you know what? Often, it didn't work. In fact, some of my advice and help made them feel worse.

Why? Because, first of all, I didn't understand their pain. And, second, because I didn't understand that my "advice" was really blaming them for their pain. To pain I was adding shame. Oh, yes, I was making things worse. Once shame comes into the picture, people just clam up and withdraw. They can learn to handle their pain, but when shame is added to it, it becomes almost impossible to bear.

And so I decided to take a new approach. I would be real. I told those who were in pain that I didn't have all the answers. In fact, I said that I didn't have *any* answers. I told them that I just wanted to understand who they were and what they were going through. I tried to listen deeply, and I tried to imagine how I would feel if I were in their circumstances. And, do you know what happened as I did that, as I gave up the feeling of needing to be the all-knowing doctor who could cure them? They began to get better! They began to say, "I feel better after talking to you because you seem to understand," or "I feel better talking to you because I can tell you care." And often they said, "I have told you things I have never told anyone else. I feel a burden has been lifted from me."

Well, that was fine as far as they were concerned, but meanwhile, I was becoming increasingly distressed about what I was doing from a scientific perspective. "Understanding," I thought, "What is that? 'Bedside manner'? 'A good personality'? 'Being *nice*'?" Spiritually based principles and intuition were guiding me more than science. Even though people seemed to benefit from what I was doing, I was unsettled. I am a scientist by training, and I felt clueless. So, as I continued to empathize with people who were in pain, I began to study, read, go to conferences, and search for answers in science. Why did my empathy for people seem to help alleviate their pain? Which aspects of the relationship were having an impact, and in which parts of the body, mind, or emotions was this impact being felt? Could one observe this impact and measure it?

My questions took me on a journey that led me in many directions. I will not bother you with all the details of my search, but I will tell you that about ten years into the journey, it began to be clear to me that what helped people was the sense that I was emotionally connected to them and that I cared, really cared about them. But, scientifically speaking, that was of no help to me, either. Egads! Caring! That is not science. And one thing is for sure, science is gospel, right? Every night on the news, the latest scientific discoveries are proudly announced. Never have I heard a newscaster say, "And now, startling news from the National Institute of Mental Health: being nice and having understanding has been proven to change people's brains in ways that reduce emotional pain, depression, isolation, and hopelessness. Niceness decreases violence in all people, of all ages, in all cultures. And that's the news for tonight."

No, I haven't heard that yet. But three years ago I heard a scientist present evidence that paves the way for such a newscast. I heard the neuroscientist Dr. Allan Schore talk about changes in a newborn baby's brain that occur as a result of the *relationship* between the mother and the baby! Aha! At last, I had found the missing piece—scientific evidence that relationships change your brain! The beginning of scientific proof that niceness, shall we say, does different things to your insides than blame or shame. Here was scientific proof that violence hurts the body and the mind and the beginning of an explanation of why therapy that is warm, caring, and empathic makes a difference—a physical difference—that is real and potentially long lasting.

The information that Dr. Schore presented has been made possible by developments in neuroimaging machines that can literally watch the brain as it functions. Striking positive physical changes are observed in the brains of infants exposed to warm and caring relationships—those that he calls "attuned"—versus the brains of infants exposed to relationships that are not attuned. Attunement fosters the development of the brain in ways that ultimately lead to a healthy emotional life. Furthermore, correlated changes are observed not only in the baby, but in the caregiver too. These attuned relationships are mutually beneficial! So, niceness matters, and now I have the scientific evidence to prove it!

In addition to Dr. Schore's work, many studies were pouring out of the new area of science called psychotraumatology, which is the science of trauma and violence. Studies in this area reinforce the notion that no real division exists between body, mind, and emotion. Traumatic relationship experiences can live on and on within the body, affecting all aspects of a person's life—their feelings, their thoughts, their physical health, their ability to form relationships—everything. Furthermore, recent research shows that unresolved trauma and loss can be passed unconsciously from one generation to the next. There is so much to learn about all of these new developments. Science, for the first time, is turning its attention away from the study of thought and cognition to the more murky, mysterious, and exciting land of emotions.

In the chapters that lie ahead, a number of popular ideas about the self, about relationships, or about healing are examined. Each of these ideas is false. I call these popular ideas myths. They confuse and distort the nature of relationship connection. Relationships, especially those we have with family and intimate friends, can provide a source of comfort, security, and positive self-esteem, or they can cause serious harm and traumatic injury. Relationships alter the course of our lives in fundamental and often unconscious ways.

As the six myths are examined, some of life's most important and challenging questions will be explored. What does it mean to "bond" to another human being? How does this bond change both individuals? Can such a bond come to an end? What is empathy, and why is it important? What does empathy do to the body, the mind, and the emotions? What about traumas such as abuse, neglect, or abandonment? Why do they leave such long-lasting scars? Why do bad memories keep repeating themselves? How do we heal? And what about the spiritual questions of life? How can we understand suffering and loss?

The old mechanistic views of life that regard man as a machine seem to turn many of life's most fundamental questions into a big boomerang. Throw out a question such as "What is life about?" and it comes boomeranging back at you. Life is about you! "You've got to go it alone." "Happiness is about making the right choices." Are past injuries bothering you? "Why don't you just get over it? It's all in your head." "Just put the past behind you and move on." And if all that doesn't work, "You have no one to blame but yourself." These myths leave those who are suffering from relationship trauma at a dead end.

Rather than turning to the self alone for healing, those who have suffered harmful relationships need to have healing relationships with others in order to move forward in life. This fact is based on the biology of the human brain and emotional system. As you read, you will learn some fundamentals about how relationships literally change your brain.

Chapter 1, "Relationships and the Living Brain," challenges the widespread, culturally accepted myth that people and their brains are basically like computers. This faulty metaphor distorts the truth of our selves. We humans are nothing like machines! Machines are dead, inorganic. We humans are alive and constantly changing, adapting, and growing ourselves "around" new experiences. As you read, you will learn that your experiences from your first day on the planet have been constantly changing the way your brain is organized. You will learn that this process of growth and change does not end when you reach adulthood, but continues throughout the lifespan. Your life is a never-ceasing process of recreating yourself.

Chapter 2, "Attunement," explains that the roots of emotional control lie in early relationship experiences with our caregivers during infancy and early childhood development. You will see that your own personality and way of relating with others began within the patterns established with your primary caregivers. This chapter challenges the myth of the isolated self. It explains that humans are biologically predetermined to be in relationships. Life is not a process of "going it alone."

Chapter 3, "Attachment," challenges the myth that you can simply think your way to happiness. You will learn that secure and insecure attachment patterns are formed in early childhood, and you will learn about their incredible impact on later life. You will see how these patterns are passed from one generation to another in unconscious, emotion-based ways of relating that do not rely on thoughts and words.

Chapter 4, "Stress, Trauma, and Memory," challenges the myth of memory, which is the idea that old traumatic memories should not be so troublesome since they are "just memories." Sufferers are often told to "just get over" their old problems because they are "in the past." This chapter discusses memory formation and how new experiences can transform old memories. It contrasts everyday stress and "normal" memory processing with traumatic memories. Information about the role of the body as a guide and basis for healing trauma will be presented.

Chapter 5, "Harnessing the Power of Relationship to Heal Emotional Pain," challenges the myth of the single cause and the quick fix—the idea that if you can identify what's wrong emotionally, you should be able to fix it quickly. This chapter explains the difference between simple trauma and complex trauma and discusses the associated healing journey. A four-stage model of healing is presented that explains the way symptoms of trauma are manifested during the various phases of healing. Suggestions to promote healing are offered.

Chapter 6, "Belief, Blame, and God," challenges the idea that God is like a vending machine doling out good stuff to the righteous and bad stuff to the bad. It challenges the belief that victims of traumas, accidents, losses, and other negative life experiences are to blame for being victims. It discusses the complexity and meaning of suffering in light of both spiritual wisdom and scientific research on false attributions.

Chapter 7, the conclusion, discusses the implications of this work. It urges the reader to grasp the core idea of the interconnectedness of all of us on planet earth. It discusses how both relationship trauma and relationship healing processes reverberate through our culture. It urges readers to realize that when you make efforts to heal from your own injuries, others are healed too. When you help another person to heal, you bring blessings to yourself.

So, who should read this book? If you are in emotional pain, you should definitely read this book, and you should give it to people in your family, to your friends, and to your health care professionals. This book will help you understand yourself, and it will help others understand you. If you have suffered emotional, sexual, or physical trauma, this book will give you a new understanding of the nature of your problems and the pathway to healing. Your new understanding will be grounded in the science of the brain and will open the door to many surprising avenues to healing.

If you have difficulties in relationships, read this book. It will explain that the formation of a secure attachment style in infancy literally "sets you up" for future healthy relationships, while the formation of insecure patterns can make future relationships difficult for you. These attachment patterns are usually unconscious. The book will help you to identify your own attachment style and help you find ways to create safe, secure, supportive relationships.

If you gobble up self-help books, watch television talk shows, or read magazines that give advice on health, please read this book.

Many people feel that there is "something wrong with them," and they don't know what it is. They have tried all the self-help tips they can find and yet remain unfulfilled, empty, and frustrated with themselves. Too much failed self-help advice can increase a sense of personal powerlessness and shame. Read this book to find out how biology plays a part in your ability to carry out "good advice."

If you are a parent, you should read this book to appreciate the remarkable, subtle, and largely hidden dance of love and attachment that takes place between you and your child. You will be amazed to discover how your child literally "borrows" your emotional control system in the first year and "grows" his or her brain "around" you as you and your child "attune." You will learn that lack of attunement can have lifelong negative consequences for your child. And, as you learn about the close connection between your emotional health and your child's, you will become much more motivated to be as healthy and happy as you can be.

If you are a member of one of the helping professions, please read this book. It will empower you to use the deepest, most authentic parts of yourself to touch the hearts of those you help. It will help you realize that the most complete, most scientifically sound and efficient way of healing is grounded in authentic relationships for which spiritual traditions are the best guide. It will give you ammunition against bureaucratic systems that all too often define success as speed, equate rigor with cold and emotionless distance, and confuse the sacred healing journey with money and the bottom line.

And finally, if you want to understand yourself and others better, please read this book. But beware! As your myths about the brain, the body, and relationships are dispelled, you may find that aspects of your whole world view are changing!

# Chapter 1

# Relationships and the Living Brain

LET ME BEGIN BY TELLING YOU A STORY ABOUT MYSELF. The story is true. I was born a twin. My brother, who was named Michael, passed away of unknown causes three days after our birth. I suspect he may have had a heart defect, because I had one—a leaky aortic valve. For some strange reason, the doctors did not discover this defect until I was about five years old. My mother took me to the doctor for a sore throat and a cold and was told that I had contracted rheumatic fever. The diagnosis was based on the doctor's sudden perception of the heart murmur, which I later found out had to have been a structural defect present from birth. I was put to bed for a full year to "recover" from rheumatic fever. Obviously, I was not going to be able to reverse a birth defect. My heart murmured when they put me to bed, and it was murmuring as loudly or more so when I was finally allowed out of bed. The story of how I finally escaped from permanent bed rest at the age of five is a vivid example of the power of relationship to bring healing, sometimes in the most unexpected of ways.

My mother's implementation of the doctor's orders of complete bed rest included months and months of lying in bed. During my convalescence my mother gave birth to another set of twins, again a boy and a girl. She became a very busy woman caring for two infants and a convalescing five-year-old child. I stayed in a rather dimly lit upstairs bedroom most of the day and waited for those moments when my mother had time to spend with me. She checked on me often, but, nevertheless, there were long periods of time when I had nothing to do. I was extremely bored. I learned to sleep a lot to pass the time. As time went on and I became more and more bored, I slept more and more.

I visited the doctor once a month for a shot of penicillin and a check on my progress. Each month my mother told the doctor that my condition seemed to be worsening because I was sleeping all the time and appeared to have no energy at all. This went on for the better part of a year, with the amount of time I spent sleeping increasing along with my mother's worry about me and her growing conviction that surely I was at death's door. The more she worried, the more vigilant she became in her efforts to keep me motionless. Eventually, I was not allowed even to walk to the bathroom. My parents carried me back and forth. That I remember vividly.

I am not sure how all of this would have ended had it not been for the arrival one day of a perfect stranger bearing a big, colorfully wrapped box full of the most peculiar looking contraptions. The box was covered in blue paper and sealed tightly. It was bigger than a bread box, but not much. Out of the top of the box tiny plastic fish were suspended over the top of holes that had been cut in the box top. The fish were tied to strings that extended into the box. If you pulled on a fish, its string emerged from the box with a tiny little toy attached to it. There were thirty such fish, a whole month's worth. I was told to pick one fish each day. The little "ocean full of fish" toy had been made by a young girl in the neighborhood, someone I didn't know and still to this day do not know. I wish I could find her and thank her for her kindness. I am convinced it changed my life. Here is what happened.

This fish box gave me something to look forward to each day. I became excited and interested and curious about the box and what might be in it. I also had some new little toys to play with each day, which, of course, kept me more awake than I had been previously. About midway through the month, I had a doctor visit, and I heard my mother tell the doctor that she thought I was getting better because I seemed more awake and peppy. "Aha!" I thought. I was a pretty smart little five year old. If peppy was "getting better," you can bet my mother saw more and more "pep" as that month wore on. Even after the toys in the fish box were gone, I made it a point to say something funny or show some signs of feeling good whenever my mother was around. Soon she decided that I would be better-off sitting in a lounge chair in the kitchen instead of being stuck all alone in a room all day while she cared for the twins. Well, you bet your life, now she saw real "pep." Little by little I inched my way out of that lounge chair and back into life. My mother had faith in her instincts. I was clearly "getting better" even if the doctor didn't think much had changed. He finally agreed to let her use her own judgment as long as I was closely watched for any signs of "overdoing it."

Years passed, and my heart condition, of course, remained. I did indeed watch it carefully and tried to heed the doctor's advice not to physically "overdo it." At forty years of age, however, the defective valve had to come out. In less than a week in the hospital the old valve was replaced by a brand new Teflon-coated St. Jude's valve that sounds like an old clock ticking if you hold your ear to my chest at just the right angle. I recovered from the surgery quickly and now enjoy a level of energy and good health I never knew was possible. My children say they could never be fooled by a "fake" mother. I am the only one who ticks like a clock!

So you see, I am a believer in science. It saved my life. And you can also see that I am aware of the limits of science and the power of relationship. This power also saved my life.

Another thing I learned when I was five was the power of prayer. My mother had taught me that I could "talk to God" by "saying my prayers." Since I had all that time alone in bed, I did plenty of talking. When the girl with the fish box turned up out of the blue, I was convinced she was an answer to my prayers. All I could see at the time was a nice box of toys, and that seemed like answer enough to a five-year-old! Little did I know that in retrospect, this little box of toys would represent a much bigger gift—a gift that changed my whole life, I think. I was convinced then that prayers are answered, and I continue to be so convinced. But now I know that the answer to our prayers is not always what we expect. Life, as I look at it now, half a century later, seems to be a constant series of spiritual challenges and marvelous surprises.

I want to share with you my understanding of how science, God, and relationship all interact in ways that can be miraculous. I want to share my understanding that there is no real conflict between science and religion. Truth is truth. But we humans are always in the process of discovering truth, of seeing only parts of it or seeing only certain angles of it, like the doctor who said I had a heart condition (which I did) and that it came from rheumatic fever (which it didn't) and that I should rest (which is fine to a point, but too much of it will kill you). And so I was saved by a "fish box" full of toys and a relationship with someone I hardly even knew. Isn't life amazing?

Ever since I started writing this book and talking about the ideas in it, people have been asking me, "How long did it take you to write your book?" I usually answer, "About thirty years." Then I laugh and smile and say, "Well, thirty years to learn the ideas and synthesize them and about a year to put it on paper." And that is the truth. In so many ways this book is a synthesis of questions about life that began when I was five and have continued throughout my career as a psychologist. Throughout all of these years, I have seen "miracles" when science and relationships with others and with God combine forces to bring about amazing change. But I am getting ahead of myself. Let's begin by meeting one of the miracles. Her name is Kim, and you will hear her story throughout the book.

# Kim

Kim is an amazing woman whom I have known for about twelve years. I am a psychologist in private practice and have established a reputation as someone who treats "difficult cases." I met Kim after the third time she tried to kill herself. She had put her head in an oven and turned on the gas. She came to see me after she had gotten out of the hospital. The first day I saw her, she said nothing and just stared at the floor. The second time I saw her she did the same thing. The third time, ditto. In fact, I saw Kim for a whole year before she was able to raise her eyes from the floor and look at me.

During that year, she wrote in a journal, which she brought to our sessions and allowed me to read silently in her presence. The journal reflected the depth of her suffering and the agony of a life that felt out of control. Her emotional pain was so great that she once wrote, "I wish I could just take my head, unscrew it like a light bulb from a socket, and screw on a new head. This one is broken—permanently!" Despite the depth of pain expressed in her writing, Kim remained silent during the entire first year that we spent together. She would bring me her writings, I would read them silently in her presence, and then I would speak, ever so gently, about what I had read. During the second year, she let me read the journal aloud, and by the third year she could look at me sometimes and talk. Today this woman is a top-selling salesperson for one of the biggest car dealerships in America!

The road to healing has been long, yes, and not without setbacks. But Kim, who came to me damaged from years of neglect, abuse, abandonment, and trauma, has healed over time. Throughout this book, I will be talking about Kim, relating her story and her healing process to the scientific ideas I will be talking about. Kim can be an inspiration to us all. No matter what your problem, no matter how much pain you feel now, you, too, can heal the way Kim has. As you read this book, I want you to keep her in mind. Keep in mind that miracles can and do happen, but usually not the way we think they should. They don't happen suddenly, with great fanfare and publicity. Often they happen slowly over time, silently, unseen, little by little, the way raindrops fill rivers.

# Why Won't My Brain
# Do What I Want It To Do?

Many people who suffer from emotional pain share Kim's feeling of being broken, damaged, permanently unfixable. They, like Kim, often complain that their emotions just won't do what they want them to do. They, like Kim, have asked me, "Why do I sometimes feel and act 'crazy'?" "Why do my emotions get out of control?" "Why do I explode with anger when I am telling myself to be patient?" "Why am I anxious when I need to be calm?" "Why can't I sleep?" "Why am I addicted to . . . (you name it)?" "Why can't I make myself be the way I *want* myself to be?"

When people like Kim ask me such questions, I answer them something like this: "Your emotions are causing you pain because you have been injured. You are hurt, and you need to heal. Just like when you break your leg, or suffer a wound in a war, you are not the same as before the injury. But that does not mean you cannot heal. You can, you will, you do heal from emotional injuries. But this healing, like all healing, takes time.

> *Knowledge and compassion for yourself can*
> *help to speed the healing process.*

Your healing will happen within our work together, within this relationship between you and me that I call the 'healing relationship.' But remember, just like a broken leg or a wound from war, the healing will happen gradually and in stages. There is no Maytag repairman for your emotional tangles. Your brain and emotional system include all of you: your body, mind, emotions, relationships, experiences, *everything*. There is no switch that can be flipped so that you will snap out of your problems. You are not a computer that simply needs to be reprogrammed by popping out old software and popping in new software. Your emotional being is an aspect of the totality of you, and you are a part of creation, a part of nature."

*"You are alive and constantly in a state of growth and renewal. You will heal. Together, you and I will walk the healing journey, and you will heal."*

## Disease or Not a Disease—Injury or Not an Injury

One of the reasons Kim believed that her brain was like a broken computer was that she had been told by some of her doctors that if she took medicine, it would cure her. She was given lots and lots of medications before, during, and after all of her attempts to hurt herself. She had the idea that medicine was the "Maytag repairman" of her brain problems. Find the right medicine, and voila! Your brain is fixed! The problem is that this solution only works for some problems. It works for problems that fit the "disease" model of mental illness. Doctors rely on a method of reasoning called "the medical model." The medical model says that to treat a disease, you must find the right diagnosis and then apply the right remedy. This should cure the disease. For example, if you have an ear infection, you take an antibiotic, it kills the infection, and you are better. Or if you have diabetes, you take insulin, and although you won't cure the diabetes, you will control it. Right diagnosis, right remedy, right treatment for the disease.

In mental health, the medical model continues to work well for mental illnesses that are disease based. For example, if you have schizophrenia, you should take medicine and realize that without it, you cannot expect to be well. This is because schizophrenia is a disease in the same sense that diabetes is a disease. Although it can't be "cured" with medicine in the sense of making it go away completely, it can usually be well controlled with medication. It is inherited and has a documented biological cause. Treating the disease of schizophrenia with a medication fits the medical model very well and, in fact, works very well. Likewise, if you have a biologically based mood disorder such as major depression or manic-depressive illness, mood-stabilizing medications and antidepressants usually work very well. There are many other mental health problems that fit the medical model well. For these problems, proper diagnosis and treatment by a psychiatrist are very important.

A psychiatrist is a medical doctor, meaning he or she trained in medical school just like your family doctor did. All doctors, from surgeons to gynecologists to psychiatrists, receive four initial years of medical training. Then, during their next three years of training, they focus on their respective fields. Psychologists do not attend medical school. They attend graduate school for approximately the same seven-year period that it takes to become a physician, but instead of studying medicine they study psychology and psychotherapeutic processes. Psychiatrists, as medical doctors, are licensed to prescribe medication. Psychologists (and other psychotherapists such as social workers and counselors), for the most part, are not licensed to prescribe medication.

However, the problems that I will be discussing in this book are not well understood by using the medical model. The problems I am discussing are related to injuries sustained within relationships and to the long-term consequences of these injuries on the brain and nervous system. In other words,

*This book is about how relationships*
*change your brain.*

A relationship injury or an emotional scar is not a disease process.

Table 1
Making a Distinction between Major Mental
Illness and Emotional Injury

EMOTIONAL INJURY

|  |  | *Yes* | *No* |
|---|---|---|---|
| MENTAL ILLNESS | *No* | 1. No mental illness, but has a history of emotional injury. | 2. No mental illness, no emotional injury. |
|  | *Yes* | 3. Has mental illness and a history of emotional injury. | 4. Has mental illness but no history of emotional injury. |

1. I have no major mental illness, but I do have a history of emotional injury. Much of what this book discusses applies to me.
2. I have neither mental illness nor a history of emotional injury. I can learn how to help others by reading this book.
3. I have both a major mental illness and a history of emotional in-

jury. While I can learn a great deal about part of my problem by reading this book, I will not learn about the parts of my problem that my psychiatrist needs to treat.

4. I have a major mental illness but no history of emotional injury. I can learn from this book, but I must remember this book does not directly address many of the problems I have.

This book is about box number 1.

To make these distinctions clearer, see Table 1. At the side of the table is the category "mental illness," with two choices: either "yes" or "no." At the top of the table is the category "emotional injury," with the choices "yes" or "no." This creates four possible groups of people: (1) people who have emotional injury but no mental illness, (2) people who have neither mental illness nor any history of emotional injury, (3) people who have mental illness and also have a history of emotional injury, and (4) people who have mental illness but no history of emotional injury. This book is about helping people who fall into box number 1.

My point in making all of these distinctions is to be clear about two things. First of all, this book is *not* about mental illness per se. Please do not interpret anything I say about healing from emotional injury as a suggestion either that mental illness is not real or that it can be cured by good relationships alone. This is not the case. Mental illness is very real and is best treated by skilled physicians. The second reason is to make clear that it is very possible to have a mental illness *and* emotional injuries. In fact, it is very common. It is also possible to have a problem with addictions and to have this problem in combination with emotional injuries and mental illness. I will mention some of this interplay later. But for now, it is enough to know that this book is about how relationships, both good and bad, affect your development. Much will become clear as the chapters unfold and one idea builds upon the next. And now on a related note . . .

# Depression, Depression, or Depression?

The English language sometimes makes it difficult to communicate about emotional things. For example, take depression. If you look at the four boxes in Table 1 and think about it, "depression" could fit in all four boxes. You can feel depressed because of a disease of major depression, or you can feel depressed as a symptom of emotional injury. Or you could be depressed as in box number 3, because of a combination of the two. You might also have neither of these problems and be depressed as a result of some physical illness or because of grief or loss. To make matters even more confusing, we sometimes use the word "depression" to describe everyday sadness, the feeling of being "bummed out," or "down" for a short time. The word "depression" is just about as confusing as the word "love" in our culture. We say we "love" ice cream, and we "love" God! How can that be the same? We "love" our parents, and we "love" the Red Sox. We "love" to sleep, and we "love" to serve humanity. And so it is with depression. We say we are "depressed" on a bad hair day, and at the other end of the spectrum, depression can be a life-threatening mental illness. Feeling sad, blue, and low in energy are signs that *something is wrong*. Temporary sadness or a low mood that is a reaction to everyday life problems will pass in a short time.

*Sadness that becomes prolonged
and interferes with daily life
may indicate a more serious problem
that warrants professional treatment.*

When in doubt, seek the advice of your family doctor. Symptoms of major depression include persistent feelings of sadness or anxiety, or loss of interest or pleasure in usual activities, plus five or more of the following symptoms over a period of at least two weeks:

- changes in appetite that result in losses or gains not due to dieting
- insomnia or oversleeping
- loss of energy or increased fatigue
- restlessness or irritability
- feelings of worthlessness or inappropriate guilt
- difficulty thinking, concentrating, or making decisions
- thoughts of death or suicide or suicide attempts

If you are suffering from these kinds of symptoms, see your family doctor.

This book is about problems that fall into box number 1 in the table—problems that are related to emotional injury rather than to a mental disease process or an addiction.

# The Brain

If we were to look in an anatomy book for a picture of the brain, we might find something that looks like Figure 1, and it would be labeled "The Brain."

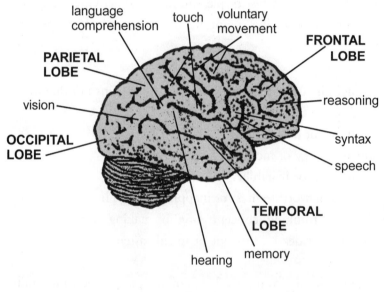

Fig. 1
The Brain

But if we could actually look inside Kim's head, we would see that this dead, static, one-dimensional picture in the textbook in no way captures the truth of Kim's living brain. As I said, it is not a dead mechanical device. It is a living aspect of all the wild and rumbling activity that is Kim in action.

*"Using your brain" is not just thinking or solving problems. It is also breathing, and feeling, and walking, and knowing which way is up. It includes feeling angry and falling asleep.*

So Kim's brain is Kim living life. It is the huge spider web of interrelated systems and processes always responding and adapting to everything that happens inside of her, everything that happens around her, and everything in between. Kim's brain is changing all the time as she moves through her day. Her brain never stops even for a second to become frozen into a picture like Figure 1.

*No, life is not like a snapshot, a moment frozen in time. Life is a three-dimensional movie, and you are the star!*

You are always experiencing things: interacting with someone, doing something, resting, working. Even when you sleep, your brain is processing. You dream. You relive the day's happenings. You relive the past. Even when you are asleep, the brain process never stops. In fact, if it does stop, you stop. That is the clinical definition of death: no brain activity.

## Don't Bore Me with "The Brain"

Now, for the most part, few subjects are apt to send the reader into a deep sleep as fast as topics that begin with the phrase "neuro-" anything. Neurology, neuroanatomy, neuroscience, and so forth.

But I promise I am not going to bore you with scads of information about neurology. I will provide some references at the end of the book for readers who want more detailed information, but mainly I am going to try to talk about the brain in a way that is simple and makes sense. You need to understand some basic facts about how brain processes happen and about how relationships are intertwined with this process.

## You Are Getting on My Nerves

People always say, "You are getting on my nerves!" What are these nerves all about, anyway? Take a look at the picture of a neuron, or nerve cell, in Figure 2. Notice that it has a pretty funny shape. It is like a long hose with a pancake at one end and a glove at the other.

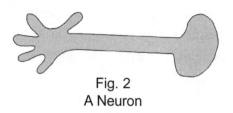

Fig. 2
A Neuron

That is just one cell. Within that cell, down the length of the "hose," electrical energy travels, and it is this electrical part of the nervous system that has given people ideas about the brain's being "wired." The problem is that this hose or wire only connects one end of one cell with the other end of the same cell. The hoses don't connect to other hoses. No sir. For one nerve cell to connect with another nerve cell something quite different has to happen—something that has nothing to do with electricity.

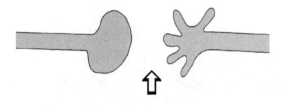

Fig. 3
The Synapse

When the electricity flows down the hose from the pancake to the glove, it causes a reaction in the glove structure that makes it release chemicals into the space between that glove and the next neuron's pancake. For the next neuron to "fire," or make electricity run down itself from one end to the other, a chemical communication has to happen between the two neurons. This is the "chemical" process in the brain, and it is this process that leads to the oft-repeated idea that people with mental illnesses have "chemical imbalances" in their brains. This is just another way of saying that their brains are not working correctly. So one neuron communicates with another neuron with chemicals. The chemicals float around in a space in the brain called a synapse. When the chemicals are in the synapses, they may or may not cause other nerves to fire.

## A Mess of Neurons

A key to understanding how the living brain works is the concept that there are so many, many, many neurons in your brain that have the potential for communicating with so many, many, many

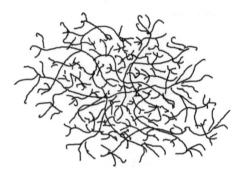

Fig. 4
A "Mess" of Neurons

others. The neurons are not arranged in your brain in neat, tidy lines, or ropes, or "wires." On the contrary, the brain is made up of billions of nerve cells that are smashed into a small space, which allows for many possibilities for "hooking up" in various and sundry ways.(See Fig. 4.)

## Order in the Chaos

But, of course, there must be some kind of order to all of this. If the nervous system were not organized, we wouldn't be able to keep our heart beating regularly and our breathing rhythmic. We also

#581  02-01-2017 8:52PM
n(s) checked out to p16470126.

The anatomy of human destructiven
: 32405000098312
TE: 02-22-17

It's not your fault : how healing
E: 32405003413617
TE: 02-22-17

ll Memorial Library  781-769-0200
ttp://www.norwoodlibrary.org

. If any old neuron could hook
l, that just wouldn't work.

*rovides order.*

bout order, but, to keep things
st two: order that is changeable
you build a skyscraper—for ex-
—you want to create a fixed or-
building changing from day to
*ucture,* and, in fact, we call the
building itself a structure. For the most part, structures are seen as
fixed in their shape and pattern.

But there is another kind of order, and this order has change
built into it. Let's take the weather, for example. The weather has
an order. It may rain or snow, but cows don't fall from the sky, and
rain never travels up. Weather is changeable, but only within certain boundaries of change. Weather, in other words, exhibits its
order in *patterns,* and, in fact, we call them weather patterns. Scientists who study weather know that it is operating according to principles and laws of nature. That is why we can sometimes predict
the weather. But the weather forecasters also know that weather
can be unpredictable, because small changes in circumstances can
have big implications for the overall weather patterns. Weather forecasters talk about the "probability" of snow or the "chances" of rain
because one may happen *if* the temperature drops, which it may
do *if* the front moves at a certain speed, but only *if . . . ,* and so on.
Weather is complex and infinitely variable. Still, we study and attempt to predict weather because within the many probable and

improbable possibilities, there is order. This is a very important concept to understand.

The brain operates according to order that is more like the weather than like the Empire State Building.

> *Your brain is constantly patterning itself*
> *in ways that are changeable.*
> *The patterns have to be changeable*
> *so that your brain can be adapting to*
> *the constantly changing circumstances of life.*

Now awake, now asleep, now threatened by a mountain lion, now in love, the brain has structures, or *patterns,* of activity and process. Try to let that idea sink in, because without understanding it, the rest of the book will make no sense. If you look in a neuroanatomy book, you will see lots of pictures of brains that will make you think they have mostly fixed structures, and that is that. But I am here to tell you that your brain is nothing like a skyscraper. You and your brain are always a work in progress! And that can be good or bad, depending on your life experiences. These experiences become part and parcel of who you are. That is what happened to Kim, as you will soon find out. She went through so many painful experiences that her insides became full of pain. But I am getting ahead of myself. It is best to start at the beginning and see how this all works.

## Unconscious Nerve Patterns

As you learn and grow, patterns of neuron cells become closely associated with each other and tend to "fire" together in established patterns. Let me give you an example. Think about driving your car. Do you have to think every time you put your foot on the brake, or do you find that you can be driving along, thinking of something entirely different than driving, and as you come to a red light, your foot just seems to travel to the brake on its own? (We're assuming you are not a new driver.)

This automatic movement suggests that there is a predetermined neural pattern in place that is associated with driving. It also suggests that

*Some nervous system functions are
unconscious while some are conscious.*

If you are lost and trying to find your way to a new friend's house, you may begin to think very carefully about where to brake and turn. But if you are cruising down a familiar route to work, you are using a preset program in your mind and body.

The fact that some functions of the nervous system are conscious and some are unconscious means that we have control over some of our functions and not over others. We can control the conscious parts but not the unconscious parts. This is a key concept.

Kim, as you recall, was feeling emotionally terrible. She could not control these feelings. Here is what she wrote about that in an excerpt from her journal that I read during her "silent" period:

*When I was a kid I thought everything about me was stupid—my thoughts, my looks, my feelings—everything. Sometimes, during the school day, I would have to lay my head on the desk because I would start to cry. I was always so sad. I never felt good about myself.*

Kim realized, even as a child, that something was wrong. But she had no idea what the problem was. At the point when she began therapy, she still did not understand why she felt so terrible.

One of the first things I helped her to see was that her feelings had begun a long time ago, in childhood, as the journal entry above shows. I explained to her that the experiences she had gone through then had become "part of her" and were causing her problems now. But I was quick to explain that these problems didn't have to last forever. Even though her nervous system had formed these patterns, it was ready, willing, and able to form new and better patterns. In the scientific literature, this ability of the brain to change its patterns and networks is called "plasticity."

## The "Plastic" Brain

The brain's remarkable ability to change its structures and patterns is called "plasticity." Let me give you an everyday example of brain plasticity.

In general, the right side of your brain controls the movement of your arms and legs on the left side of your body. The nerves "cross over," as it were. If you have a stroke and damage the right side of your brain, for a while you will have trouble moving your left leg. However, after a while, you will be able to relearn to move that leg. Those neural patterns in your brain will reorganize themselves according to the new demands of the situation. After a time of practice, you will walk again! So the brain has the ability to organize into patterns and to *reorganize* those patterns according to the changing demands of the environment. The ability of the right side of your brain to control your left leg was programmed by your genes. Then the right side of your brain was damaged. And yet, under the press of extreme environmental circumstances, the brain was able to adapt to the new situation.

A word about genes. You are born with certain dispositional temperaments, capacities, and potential that come about through heredity. No question about it. These genetic predispositions set you up to have certain capacities and temperaments that emerge when the time and circumstances are right. But genes are not a blueprint chiseled in stone that determines who you are and how you will behave. On the contrary, scientists are beginning to believe that experience plays a much bigger role in the ultimate outcome of a human being than they had previously thought.

*Much more of who you are*
*is not genetically predetermined*
*but is rather the result of*
*the interaction over time*
*between the forces of nature*
*and the forces of experience.*

This is another concept Kim struggled with. In one of her journal entries she writes:

*Why do I keep going back to Dr. Pat for help? She can't help me. No one can. I was born wrong. I am crazy. I always knew I was, even when I was little. I never felt right. My head never stops. It's just the way I was made, that's all. I've always been this way, and I'll always be this way. That is just the way it is.*

You can see the machine-built-wrong way of thinking here. "I was born wrong" means "I was built wrong by genes from the beginning." Part of what I had to explain to Kim was that genes are only part of the story. Everyone has genes, yes, and everyone is influenced by the various traits, skills, and characteristics they inherit. But so much of what lies inside of us in our genes cannot be manifested unless we have all the things around us that we need to express it.

*We need people to care about us and to connect with us.*

You will read more about this in the next chapter.

# Cutting-Edge Science

In science the debate about how much of who we are comes from our genes and how much comes from our experience has been called the "nature versus nurture" controversy. Some scientists on the nature side said that you are born with a basic gene structure (skyscraper-type organization) that sets the growth pattern for who you are to become, and that's that. So genes were thought to be the architectural plans for the structure of you. From this point of view, you may get bigger as you grow because genes are programmed for growing, and you may learn things and have various experiences, but these experiences won't alter the basic structure of your brain. This is the viewpoint that Kim was expressing—made wrong, and that is that. If this were true, Kim's case would be hopeless. But this is machine talk again—the genes build the machine, and the machine runs the way it is built. That is not the way it is.

*Is it*
**NATURE?** ⇨ THAT MAKES **ME?**
*OR*
**NURTURE?** ⇨ THAT MAKES **ME?**

**NATURE?**

**NURTURE?**

IT'S BOTH
NATURE & NURTURE
INTERACTING

NURTURE AND NATURE AND NURTURE AND NATURE AND NURTURE AND NATURE AND NURTURE AND

Fig. 5
Nature versus Nurture

Scientists on the other side of the old debate took an equally extreme but opposite position. They said no, experiences make you who you are. In fact, everyone's brain is like a blank slate, and the differences between people are due to their different experiences. So from this point of view, Kim may have gotten "messed up" from her experiences, but the fact that she stayed messed up was her fault. She should have created new experiences by now to change herself into the person she wants to be. According to this point of view, the thing to do is to start thinking differently about yourself—to start "reprogramming the computer" with positive thoughts. Well, for Kim, that didn't work at all. She found her thoughts so confused most of the time that it was impossible to control them. Forget using her thoughts to control her emotions.

So if we were to stick with the machine metaphor, Kim was doomed. Either she was programmed incorrectly by her genes and was permanently "broken," or she should have been able to "reprogram" herself by thinking different thoughts, an assignment that she knew from personal experience was impossible. I explained to her that these dead-end views do not coincide with the new understanding that genes and experience interact in an organic way. The two processes cannot be separated. They are different aspects of the same unified process of being alive and being Kim, or being you. The interaction of these two processes may create good feelings or emotional pain. It all depends on the experiences and how they become part of who you are.

So, believe it or not, you now have an understanding of the brain that opens the door for you to be on the cutting edge of the newly emerging understanding of how your brain is constantly recreating itself in the context of new experiences. With the understanding that nerve cells operate in patterns and networks in response to demands from genetics and experience, you are on the road to understanding yourself and others in a whole new way.

From this point of view, it is clear why Kim was having so much trouble. Her brain had "grown around" the unrelenting traumas and negative emotional experiences. Genetically, Kim had been born with many gifts that became evident as her healing process unfolded. But her negative emotional experiences had not allowed her full potential to blossom.

*Experience—especially emotional experience—plays a major role in bringing what is potential into reality.*

As chapter 2 explains in detail, your relationship experiences in early life change the structure of your brain and, therefore, how your brain works. It is necessary to grasp this in order to understand the power of relationships in your own life today. Realize that even now, even as you read this book, you are changing your brain patterning. You are changing as a result of what you are reading. In education we call this change "learning." But learning is not just a process of acquiring new thoughts and ideas. There is a more powerful, more fundamental learning that is emotional. This is the first learning—the learning of the infant. This is the learning that stays with you and influences you profoundly in ways that are both conscious and unconscious. And this dynamic structure-changing process is not over. It is continuous. You are still changing who you are and how you brain works as you interact with life experiences and especially as you have relationships.

# Summary

Despite what you may have read in books or learned in school, your brain and nervous system are not like a computer or any other kind of mechanical device. But this information is relatively new to our culture. In fact, this news made the front cover of *Time* magazine on 2 June 2003. The cover of the prestigious magazine asked the question, "What makes you *special?* Are you programmed from birth, or does life change the program? . . ." The lead-in to the article asked, "What makes you who you are? Which is stronger—nature or nurture?" and then answered its own question by stating, "The latest science says genes and your experience interact for your whole life."[1]

For *Time* magazine, this information was big news. And it really is. The implications of this new understanding of life are staggering. This new understanding means that experience changes you in ways that are much more fundamental than you might have ever thought possible. The *Time* article explains that genes themselves are not "static blueprints that dictate our destiny." Experience and genes interact in patterned ways that are more like the weather than like a skyscraper. Just as a wind change in Oklahoma can affect the rainfall in Maine, a small change in experience can have big implications in later life.

> *Your brain patterns itself in response to experiences.*
> *Relationships are powerful experiences. And so,*
> *relationships change your brain.*

In chapter 2 we will look at the subject of relationships and begin with the most important one: the relationship between mother,
father, or other caregiver and the newborn infant. The dynamics
that we will discuss begin in infancy and continue throughout the
lifespan. We will also take on the myth of the isolated self—the
myth that in life you "go it alone." This is far from the truth. If
every experience potentially changes you, and if relationships are
one of the most powerful experiences, it is clear that from the moment of conception on, you are engaged in a dance of mutual in-
terdependence with others. But let's take it from day one on the
planet. Let's begin by checking in with a newborn. Let's see how his
or her intimate relationship with a caregiver patterns the brain in
ways that will form the foundation of personality and emotional
well-being. Later in chapter 2 we will revisit Kim and see how the
things we are discussing affected not only the emotional injuries
she received, but also, and more importantly, how they affected the
process by which she healed from those injuries.

# Chapter 2

# Attunement

HAVE YOU EVER NOTICED THE WAY YOU ACT AROUND A BABY? Usually, you get up close to the baby's face, look right in the baby's eyes, and talk in a funny cooey voice. "Hello, Baby. Ohhhh, cooo." The baby gazes back, right into your eyes. If you are lucky, the baby smiles. And now you are all excited! You smile, too, still looking into the baby's eyes. Then the baby smiles even more, or maybe even coos. Now you are even more delighted. "He likes me!" you say to the friends around you, feeling pleased with yourself. Now the baby is even more animated and begins to gurgle and wave his arms excitedly. You and the baby continue the game of gazing, cooing, and smiling until the baby looks away and the game ends.

This game of interaction is called "attunement" in the scientific literature. Attunement is a good name because it captures the notion of relationship connection, of being "tuned in" to each other.

*It is interesting to look at attunement between a baby and an adult because so many things about emotional connection and relationships that hold true for adults are clearer and easier to observe when you are dealing with a baby.*

The most obvious thing about this interaction is that no conversation occurred, yet you and the baby communicated and even got excited about each other. You came away from the interaction with the sense that the baby liked you and that you liked the baby. You made a relationship connection, and yet no real words were spoken. Instead, both you and the baby made noises and, through the tone of these noises and through the smiling, gesturing, and especially the eye-to-eye gazing, you and the baby made this connection.

So what just happened between you and the baby? What was traded, transmitted, exchanged? It wasn't ideas. It wasn't thought. What was it? Let's call this baby "Matthew" and think about what is going inside his mind as you and he interact.

Think about Matthew. Can he think the way you do or speak like you? No, not at all. He didn't wake up on his first day on the planet and think to himself, "Gee, I sure need a nip of milk. I think I will cry like a banshee and see if that works." No. The ability to think and to solve problems has to develop in the brain. In fact, according to people who study child development, most people don't have their full cognitive abilities until they are about sixteen years old! So what does baby Matthew have during those early weeks and months of life? What is it that he has and that you have, which you trade back and forth during the attunement process?

Emotions. The sounds, the tone of voice, the facial expressions, the eye-to-eye gaze communicate emotion, and the baby responds with emotion. The look on your smiling face carries an emotional message directly to baby Matthew's brain. He *feels* the message and responds with his feelings. He smiles, coos, and shakes his hands with delight.

Think about being with baby Matthew when he begins to cry. Now that baby Matthew's response has changed, what will you do? Will you continue to smile and coo at him? No, not if you are a skilled caregiver. You will immediately shift gears. Seeing the unhappy look on baby Matthew's face, your face will mirror his distress. "Ohhh, what is the matter, Baby?" you might say. "Oh, now there, it's OK. Everything is all right." You pat baby Matthew on the back, speak in a soothing voice, and give him hugs and all kinds of vocal and physical assurances that everything is OK. This feeling of comfort calms baby Matthew and restores his sense of safety. Your actions, your tone of voice, the expression on your face tell baby Matthew that everything is all right, and he absorbs that emotional message and calms down.

Notice that while this emotional attunement process was going on, you, the adult, were the one who adjusted and modulated your emotions in different ways to match the baby's needs. Notice that when the baby was happy, you did things to increase those happy feelings and make them last longer, but when he was sad, you acted in ways that reduced the strength and intensity of the negative emotions.

This concept of attunement will become very important as our discussion continues. Nothing in the world is better for baby Matthew's emotional health than attunement, which is the matching and synchronizing of emotion between individuals. By the same token, as we will discuss in chapter 3, chronic, severe misattunement can create problems that may last a lifetime. But first let's begin with the good news, which is that attunement fosters the growth of baby Matthew's brain as well as your own.

# Attunement: "Turning Up the Volume" on Positive Emotions

If baby Matthew is happy, your attunement to him is likely to make him feel even happier. The scientific literature calls this "amplification" of the emotion, which means to make the emotion stronger and more significant for the baby. For instance, when you were first looking in Matthew's eyes and he was responding, you responded and saw an increase in the delight on his face. When you saw this increase, you matched it with more delight on your part. "He likes me!" you said in an excited voice, and now your face was looking even more delighted, too. Then Matthew, feeling your increased joy and excitement, got even more excited. His joy increased. He began to make gurgling noises and waved his arms in excitement

> *Scientists tell us that these attuned interchanges are crucial for a baby's healthy emotional development.*

They have found that as this interchange goes on, the baby's brain is building the neural networks we discussed in chapter 1. The networks mirror the emotional neural networks in your brain as you and the baby interact. Your "joy" neural network becomes a template, or neural pattern, that becomes part of the baby's brain. We will discuss this more later.

# Attunement: "Turning Down the Volume" on Negative Emotions

What about the crying baby? Did attunement play a role in that interaction too? Absolutely. A baby is not born with the ability to comfort and soothe himself. His brain does not yet have the neural networks to do this. So, when baby Matthew gets upset, he needs you to comfort him so that he literally feels *your* comfort and "borrows" it to meet his own needs at the time. He feels what you feel, and in feeling it, his brain "grows around" this experience of comfort, building the comfort pathways in his little brain. Before he experiences comfort coming from you, he cannot create comfort pathways in his own nervous system. The baby's experience of comfort is being patterned from the comfort templates of *your* brain that you are unconsciously sharing with him.

## Template Learning

The process I have just described is called "template learning" in scientific literature. A template is a pattern that provides the shape and form for something that is being created. For example, if you are making a quilt, you might have a template of a triangle that you will trace onto your material and cut out, then sew together with other triangles to make the entire quilt. The template enables you to trace or copy the desired triangle shape onto your cloth.

The baby's brain is like the cloth, and the pattern of emotional responses that you are sharing with the baby is like the triangle, which shapes and forms the neural pathway that will become the baby's internal experience of joy. In the brain, the pattern is made up of the parts of the nervous system that are responsible for the body's experience of an emotion. In this case, the part of the brain that makes the face smile and the systems that release hormones to help the brain imprint these neural pathways make up the pattern. Eventually, the joy template will include a pathway that passes through speech centers, because as we know, eventually the baby will be able to say, "I am happy" or "I am so excited." But not yet, not at first. First the baby's brain becomes imprinted with neural patterns that come from his mother or other primary caregiver— you in this instance.

Another way to think about a template is to imagine the damp sand on a beach after the tide has gone out. Have you ever walked on that damp sand and looked at the imprint your foot makes with each step? The sand now has a template, or imprint, of your foot. Like the footprint in the sand, a neural template is "plastic."

The word "plastic" as it is used here means "able to change shape." If the tide comes in and washes over your footprint, the imprint may change shape or disappear altogether. If not, it may harden in the sun and become relatively firm and long lasting. The brain's template-forming capacity is like this. Templates, or structures, form in response to experiences, and these templates may be relatively transient or more long lasting, depending on a number of variables that we will discuss.

# Eye-to-Eye, Face-to-Face

"How in the world," you might ask, "can one person's brain affect another person's brain so directly? That almost sounds like science fiction, not science. My brain is going to 'stamp a template' onto someone else's brain? That sounds crazy! Everybody's brain is their own!"

Well, now, is it? That is a myth that I hope to dispel—the myth that it is every man for himself. Let's see what you think after you read on.

The neurobiologist Dr. Allan Schore has studied the neurobiology of attunement and described the attunement process in detail. We have already talked about some of his findings. Based on what we have discussed so far, one might reason that if "good" relationships make the baby feel good and, therefore, more healthy and able to "grow its *own* brain," then the absence of this comfort and support might slow things down a bit. Many people believe this. But actually, according to Schore, the influence, especially during certain stages of development called "critical periods," is much more radical and direct than that.

A critical period is a time of life when nature has preprogrammed you to learn certain things very quickly and easily and during which time the learning that takes place remains relatively permanent. Let's take an obvious example—language, for instance. You know that a child between two and five years old learns whatever language is spoken to him or her. If the language is English, you will have an English-speaking child, if it is Spanish, a Spanish-speaking child. We also know that if children whose parents speak more than one language use both languages in the home during this critical period, the child will become fluent in both. The child seems to absorb language effortlessly during this critical period. Although you can still acquire new languages later in life, it will never be as easy and automatic for you as it was during that critical period for language acquisition. The language you learn during this critical period will become relatively permanent because the learning will be recorded in the brain in language templates. These templates will form quickly during this time and will become part of the language structure of your central nervous system.

Dr. Schore explains that a similar process occurs during emotional development. The eyes are an extension of the brain—almost like a window into the brain. During periods when a mother and baby gaze at each other's eyes, their brains are in contact and communication. During this contact, the baby is able to imprint information from the mother that helps to structure its emotional system! This imprinting process creates structures—emotional templates—that become relatively permanent.

It works something like this. You and baby Matthew gaze into each other's eyes. In a physiological response to gazing at his smiling face, your pupils dilate and create a sort of glimmer or gleam in your eye. This enlargement of the pupil of your eye is like a searchlight that gets baby Matthew's attention. It orients him to pay attention to you. He gazes back at you with enlarged pupils, his eyes bright and shining. Certain parts of his nervous system that are too complicated to describe here are then sent a "Now Print!" message, which captures in that moment the look on your face and all of the emotions that accompany it. This total experience is registered in the baby's brain instantaneously. This is called a "flashbulb memory."

# Whose Emotions Are These, Anyway?

During this moment of imprinting, an emotional merger takes place. The child experiences your emotions as if they were his own, so that not only does his outward behavior match your outward behavior, but also his internal experiences match, or "merge," with your internal experiences. During an imprinting experience, not only do you and the baby smile on the outside together, but also you and the baby have the same feelings inside together. You are matching your internal states, not just your outward behaviors. The change in your internal state and in that of the baby means that the baby's nervous system is changing and creating a pattern to help make this experience happen again in the future. Once this pattern is formed, it will be easier and easier for the baby to recreate this joy experience on his own. At first, the baby cannot tell the difference between his joy and your joy. They are not differentiated. As time goes on and the internal templates form, the emotional experience of joy becomes less "borrowed" from you, less a mirror of your experience, and more and more the baby's own internal experience. This is a gradual process, the process of differentiation.

Other fascinating changes occur during attunement—changes not only in the baby's brain, but in yours as well! The experience of joy is, of course, a pleasurable one. The pleasure experience in the brain depends on the release of certain chemicals (remember the glove and the pancake from chapter 1) that give you the good feeling. The baby has the same feelings of pleasure. It will not take the baby long to realize that if he can get your attention and smile at you, you are likely to smile back, and he will have a good feeling inside. And so the baby learns to do this.

You, too, being at least as smart as the baby, realize that you get a good feeling when the baby is smiling at you. You will enjoy this process and seek it out often. The mutuality of the emotions going back and forth between you and the baby will amplify the emotions, making a small good feeling into a really big good feeling. That's why a mother looks so happy at the end of the day when her baby has been in a good mood. She's had that good feeling of pleasure all day. Of course, the opposite is also true, but we will discuss negative emotions later.

## The Survival Value of Attunement

The amazing power and strength of the emotional imprinting process is not accidental. Nature has designed these processes to ensure the baby's very survival. The neural pathways that have to do with emotional life are located in the very same parts of the brain that control the basic life functions of your body—functions such as breathing and keeping your heart beating. Think about the "survival package" that comes with the human infant when he arrives in the world. The infant has a body, and he has the ability to keep his body alive with automatic functions such as breathing and heart rate (part of the autonomic nervous system) and basic emotions that allow him to cry when he is hungry and smile when he is contented.

At first, these basic expressions of emotion are the baby's only link between himself and the world. They are messages of survival. I am hungry. I hurt. I am happy. The baby sends these emotional messages, and you, the baby's caregiver, translate them into your language and give the baby what he needs, whether it be a smile, a bottle of milk, or something else. All of the time while you are doing this, you are creating within the baby the neural pathways that will ultimately allow him to go and get his own milk, keep himself safe, and, most importantly, know and feel and name his own emotions.

*Emotion is basic to survival. Emotion tells us both what is going on inside of us and what is going on within the connections we are forming and reforming with others all the time.*

## Emotions Are in the Body

How do our emotions communicate to us? How do they communicate to others? In the body. Remember, baby Matthew does not have words, but he still communicates loudly and clearly. The body feels the emotion, and the body communicates the emotion to others who also feel these emotions within their bodies.

Somehow, in our word-heavy culture, the importance of emotion in the body has gotten rather lost. I have a dog named Maggie, and she and I communicate emotionally all the time. You should see her when she gets a new rawhide bone. She leaps up and down with glee! No one seeing her do this would mistake her behavior for anything but joy. And if she sees us packing suitcases, well, Maggie communicates then, too—sometimes in ways that require quite a bit of cleanup afterward! She tells me what she thinks about my going away and leaving her.

People are a lot smarter than dogs, but they share an emotional system that is similar in some basic ways to that of the mammals who live with us here on planet Earth. People communicate to each other all the time with their bodies, tone of voice, facial expression, and gestures. But somehow, after people learn words, they begin to rely more on those words than on what they can see, feel, and experience directly in relationship with others on an emotional level. Adults—and especially people who have experienced a lot of trauma—can become very confused emotionally. They can become "numb" to their own emotions or "dissociated"—disconnected from them. They can experience their emotions as "out of control," swinging wildly from one extreme to another.

When adults feel their emotions are out of control, they sometimes think that they should try to eliminate the emotions or suppress them to get them "in control." But, as this discussion makes clear, your emotions are actually part of your body, part of who you are. They are crucial for your survival. So, what about this issue of emotional control?

## Developing Emotional Control

The previous discussion has shown that babies are born without emotional control. We take this for granted. No one looks at a two-month-old crying baby and says, "That child needs to get his act together!"

But what do we say and think of an adult who has poor emotional control? Do we say, "Oh, that person has not had the opportunity to form an attachment with another in which he can develop his emotional control"? Or do we say, "Boy, that guy is crazy!" and blame him for being crazy? We are probably more apt to do the latter.

So there is some point in the process of development at which we stop thinking that it is OK for a person to have poor emotional control—as they do when they are born—a point when we start expecting them to have their emotions under wraps. We do not expect baby Matthew at six months of age to have emotional control. But what about when Matthew is sixteen? By that point we expect him to have this control. What takes place between six months and sixteen years inside Matthew that should, if all goes well, give him this control?

# Emotional Control: A Step-by-Step Process

We used to think that what happened in the brain to give you emotional control was just growing up and getting bigger. We thought that you were genetically programmed to have emotional control. That is why Kim said when she came to see me that she felt she was somehow made wrong because she had such poor control over her emotions. Now science is saying, "No." Science has discovered that in order for even genetically preprogrammed development to unfold optimally within a person's life, the circumstances have to be right. Without the right circumstances, the neural pathways for emotional control cannot develop properly.

What kind of circumstances do we mean? As it turns out, we mean that baby Matthew needs an emotionally attuned caregiver to bond with him so that he can develop the neural pathways that will enable him to have emotional control. Let's go back to the mother comforting her baby. Although the baby feels emotionally upset and cries, the neural pathway that enables him to cry is already in place when the baby is born because it is essential for survival. But the neural pathways needed for self-soothing and self-regulation are *not* there.

*Initially, the feeling of calm and comfort must come from his caregiver so that the baby's body and mind will feel it, attune to it, and begin to grow internal pathways in concert with that experience.*

This idea is not so farfetched if you consider how we learn something more familiar and mundane, such as how to swing a golf club. If you have ever tried to learn to play golf, you know that for most people the movement needed to hit a golf ball is not innate. Someone has to teach you and show you how to do it. It is common for the person to show you how to grip the club and then correct your attempts to mimic this grip. The person may stand behind you, swing the club with you, show you how your head should stay still while your shoulders rotate and your weight shifts, and so on. This movement will often feel very awkward at first. After lots and lots of practice, it becomes "automatic," second nature. Once you have practiced and mastered the body movements needed to hit the ball, it begins to feel very natural, like a way of moving that is so familiar that you feel as if you have always been able to hit a golf ball this way. As time goes on, you may not even remember how awkward you felt the first time you picked up a golf club. In your mind, as the neural pathways were being formed for the new "golf template," you did not know how to behave, how to act. You needed another person to mirror so that you could set your own internal control patterns in the same way. You borrowed someone else's golf template by practicing with that person until you made it your own.

Neurons had to grow in certain ways, forming various connections with other synapses in repeating patterns that soon formed a template in your mind. Once these templates were laid down, you could just swing the club without even thinking about it. It had become "natural."

People who have an emotionally attuned caregiver will develop emotional control through a process that is very much like the process I just described for learning a golf swing. At first, emotional control will be impossible, but over time, the networks and pathways that will allow it to happen "naturally" will grow and develop. The step-by-step progress of this learning curve will not be obvious. It is not conscious.

*Babies who are learning emotional control must learn one step at a time, and each step is dependent upon mastery of the step before it.*

The old adage that you have to crawl before you can walk holds true in the emotional realm, too. For example, people who do not have the ability to calm and soothe themselves often have difficulty handling the everyday problems of life. When they get upset, they stay upset and get others upset. People like this are often told they "overreact." You will learn more about this in the following chapters when we discuss the effects of trauma on emotional reactivity.


# The Unconsciousness of Attunement

Throughout your day you experience changing states within your body, your mood, and your emotions. All of these processes and all of your interactions with others—that is, all of your experiences—leave their traces on your nervous system. Some experiences—especially those that are accompanied by strong emotion—become imprinted within your neural templates. Some experiences are imprinted temporarily and then either fade away or get integrated with other information into your long-term memory stores. As all of this dynamic change and constant adjustment goes on, you are able to adjust your attention and consciousness so that, for the most part, you remain completely unaware of what is happening inside your brain. You may be aware of your behavior or even your feelings, but you are not aware of the template-forming processes in your brain. You have to infer them secondhand from your behavior and feelings.

For example, at the beginning of this chapter, when you and baby Matthew were smiling at each other, you might have realized that you were smiling at a baby, but you did not say, "Gee, I think I will go get a zap of some pleasure brain chemicals and do some neural reprogramming while I am here with this baby." No, you just did what came naturally. Even an observer watching you interact with Matthew would not know for sure what changes were going on in your brain and in the baby's brain.

Remember, we established in chapter 1 that the brain is not like a computer. There is no indicator on your forehead that lights up and says, "Reprogramming in Process." There is no crunching sound as the circuits connect, disconnect, and reconnect. There is only the flow of experience, the flow of relationship between you and others. Within this flow, each of you is changing as your experience knits your emotional systems together. Another word for this is "bonding." In chapter 3 we will discuss bonds of attachment. But first, let's look at how the attunement process can go awry and examine the consequences of what we call "misattunement."

## Misattunement: Accidentally Out of Sync

Return to the scene at the beginning of the chapter when you and baby Matthew were attuning. You and Matthew were gazing and smiling, emoting back and forth, back and forth, until he looked away and the game ended. What do you think would happen if, when baby Matthew looked away, you were to continue trying to keep him engaged in gazing and cooing? What would happen if, instead of pausing the interaction when he paused, you were to continue playing the game? This state of affairs is called "misattunement."

In attunement, you are interacting with the baby according to the pace and intensity that the baby sets. You are taking your emotional cues from baby Matthew and adjusting and pacing your expression of emotion according to what you read on his face. You are synchronizing your emotional dance. As in real dancing, someone needs to lead. In an attuned relationship with an infant, the baby is leading and you, the adult, are following.

In a misattuned interaction you are not following. You are doing something to stop the action, as it were. This might happen in many different ways. One way that it can happen is if you are in a state of attunement but fail to pace your emotions according to the baby's needs. When this happens, the interaction becomes "misattuned." If, instead of giving Matthew some time to recover from the intensity of the cooing game, you continue to try to arouse him to high positive emotion, he may become distressed. If you prolong the interaction this way, eventually he will cry. As the now misattuned caregiver, you may be mystified as to why this baby, who was laughing and smiling only moments before, is now crying. Perhaps you now continue with misattunement. Suppose you become frustrated because the baby you want to see laughing is crying instead. Perhaps you will try even harder to stimulate him emotionally by making funny faces, prodding him, or bouncing him up and down in ways that he often finds to be fun. Is this likely to help?

No. This is more misattunement. He is likely to cry even harder. Now perhaps you escalate the misattunement and scold the baby, telling him not to cry. What is likely to happen? Louder crying, right? So as you can see, misattunement will stop the flow of positive emotion and instead trigger negative emotion. Furthermore, escalating misattunement will trigger escalating distress because, as we know, baby Matthew does not have the nervous system pathways to comfort and soothe himself. This escalating misattunement makes matters worse. To calm Matthew, you would need to attune with him as described earlier.

# Misattunement: Purposefully Out of Sync

Not all misattunement is a bad thing. At times, intentional misattunement is used to stop an escalating flow of emotion that seems to be getting out of control. In fact, baby Matthew misattuned by turning his head away from you during the cooing game. This misattunement, triggered by the baby's overstimulated emotional system, did two things. It stopped the flow of emotion that was going back and forth, and it turned attention away from the relationship. As an observer, you would have been able to see this because the baby turned his head away and took his eyes off of you. Remember that the eye-to-eye contact was the way the nervous system was stamping its patterns, so when the baby turned away, this connection ended.

I have said that the attunement process is pleasurable. Why, then, would baby Matthew turn his attention away and stop the emotional flow?

*The answer is stress, believe it or not.*

Connecting emotionally is stressful. It is an intense experience. Once baby Matthew reached the limit of his ability to handle this intensity, he turned away. After reaching this limit, any more emotion, even if it were positive emotion, would be distressing to him. Too much intensity. More misattunement. Continuing to pressure him to interact with you would increase baby Matthew's stress. You probably didn't realize that you could stress out a baby. Well, you can.

As you will learn later in the book, stress for a person of any age is basically the process of "stuff" that your insides find it difficult to handle coming at you from the environment. It certainly gets more complicated than that, but basically, if you think about it, that is what stress is. When you have to go through things that your insides really *can't* handle, it is called "extreme stress." That is the topic of chapter 4.

So experiences that are too intense cause *distress*. What do I mean by intensity? Think about a color—for example, red. Now think about fire engine red, valentine red. That is really red, right? Now think about pale pink. Pink is red mixed with white to reduce the intensity. Which is a more stimulating color, and which is more relaxing? Most people would say red is an exciting color and pink is a softer, more quieting color. Both are red, but one is more intense than the other. I sometimes refer to intense red as "screaming red." Joy, excitement, and interest can be "screaming," too—very intense. When the intensity is too great, there must be a break, a rest, to make the emotional interchange pleasant. Otherwise, "screaming red" hurts!

So, to get a misattuned, "screaming-red" baby back to a "pink" calm state, you need to add the "cool white" of comfort. Eventually, the overtaxed baby will respond to your shift of gears, and your comfort will calm and soothe him. Keep in mind that the emotions are in the body. This is why rocking and hugging the baby soothes his overwrought emotions.

## Misattunement and Reattunement

Misattunement can be caused by accidentally being out of sync with your baby and failing to respond to cues to stop, shift gears, or reduce intensity. Misattunement can also happen on purpose, when we send out a competing emotion.

Let me give you an example. Fast forward to a time when Matthew is about two years old. You and he are playing with toys on the living room rug. He has a pile of little cars, and he is putting them into a big toy box sitting next to you. Each time he picks up a car to put it in the box, he shows it to you proudly and says, "Car!" You smile back at him with admiration, attuning to his pride. With each car Matthew puts in the box, his sense of pride and joy increases, and you, too, feel this happiness in your attunement with him. Suddenly, instead of putting the next car in the box, he throws the car as hard as he can, smack into your face, and grins a big, huge grin.

What do you do? Do you "attune" and smile back? Not if you are an excellent caregiver. An excellent caregiver knows when not to attune, when to deliberately misattune.

When you get hit in the face, your natural tendency is to say, "Ouch!" in an irritated voice and to grab your face. Then you might be likely to look at the grin on Matthew's face and mirror back an angry, reproachful glare. At this point you would expect Matthew to react with shame, to lower his eyes, blush, and drop his arms. He might even start to cry if the look you are giving him is particularly intense. This is purposeful misattunement on your part. By showing him the emotional consequences of this kind of action, you are teaching Matthew not to throw things in people's faces. Inside himself, Matthew feels shame, and this is a very unpleasant feeling. He won't want to feel this again if he can help it. He will be much less likely to include throwing cars into your face the next time he plays the put-the-car-into-the-box game. In this case, this is a positive use of shame to socialize and teach a child how to behave.

If you are a skilled caregiver, after a short time of letting Matthew experience the shame, you and he will return to the game of putting cars into the box and will reattune. This will be necessary because the shame experience will cause distress in Matthew, and he will not be able to return to a calm state alone any more than he could calm himself after falling down and scraping a knee or burning a finger on a stove. The shame "burns," and he will need you to reattune to him in a positive way. Matthew will again see you being proud of him, and he will have learned two important lessons, one more important than the other. He will, of course, have learned to put the cars into the box—not his caregiver's face. That is the first lesson. But the more important lesson he will have learned is that there can be misattunement followed by reattunement. He will learn that emotional distress can be followed by emotional comfort and security. He will learn that you can be upset with his behavior and not reject him. The reattunement following the misattunement helps drive this point home.

In only a few moments in time, through behavior and emotional facial expressions, some major lessons about life have been passing back and forth between you and Matthew. These lessons, like the lessons of the more simple and straightforward attunement I described earlier, will also form relationship templates in Matthew's developing brain. These two lessons will become possible relationship patterns—to attune, misattune, reattune. And no words were ever spoken.

## Shame and the Disgusted Face

Humor me for a minute. Go to the refrigerator and take out a lemon or some other really sour or bad-tasting food, then head for the nearest mirror. While looking in the mirror, take a big bite out of the food and look closely at the expression on your face as you taste it. See your eyes squint, your nose wrinkle up, your lips pucker, and the corners of your mouth turn down? It's not a pretty sight, is it? This is the face of disgust. The word itself comes from the Latin root *gustus,* as in gustatory, or pertaining to taste. If something happens to us that we feel was unjust, we say it didn't "sit right" (in our stomachs) or that we can't "stomach" that kind of thing, and it "leaves a bad taste in your mouth." This is disgust.

If you want to stop an emotionally joyful, emotion-enhancing, positively joy-accelerating moment dead in its tracks, just shoot a look of disgust at someone. Bam! Instant misattunement in a big way. If emotional attunement kicks things up a notch, shaming misattunement will kick it down ten notches.

What is "it" and what are these "notches"? Positive attunement and the resulting attachment begin to create in baby Matthew an expectation about his relationship with you. Matthew expects, or at least hopes, that when he comes around you, you are going to smile and pay attention and make him feel even better than he does already. That is "it"—the expectation of a good feeling. But if that is what Matthew expects, and if what Matthew gets is your disgusted face, then he will feel shame, and this will kick his emotional experience down many, many notches.

## Forming Skyscrapers and Weather Patterns

Another way to think about expectations in relationships is to think about the patterns mentioned in chapter 1. Remember the skyscraper kind of neural structure versus the weather-pattern kind of neural structure? Repetitive experiences of emotional communication within a relationship create neural structures.

*The more a certain pattern of relationship is repeated, the more permanent this neural structure becomes.*

For example, if you and baby Matthew attune every time you interact, baby Matthew's brain will begin to form patterns of relationship that are more like skyscrapers than like the weather. In other words, repetitive patterns create neural structures that are more permanent than the structures created by one-time occurrences. Over time, as baby Matthew attunes with you, he develops within his own nervous system something that science calls a "secure relationship attachment pattern." This will be discussed in detail in chapter 3. The important concept here is that a repetitive, comforting, attuned relationship creates healthy, more-or-less permanent neural patterning.

What does "healthy patterning" mean? In a nutshell, it means lots and lots of interconnections have been formed among all the parts of the brain. Different parts of the brain are associated with different functions. Certain areas in the brain control speech and language while others control movement and action. Still others control rational thought. A child who has had the opportunity to "grow" his or her brain within an attuned relationship will have "connected up" emotional experiences with these other brain functions. In other words, emotions will *inform* speech, language, action, and rational thought.

As time goes on, a baby in an attuned relationship will learn to recognize feelings, name them, and talk about them with others. Eventually, the child will be able to identify a feeling and take time to think about it before acting on it. That child will not be frightened of his or her own feelings but rather will welcome them as an important piece of information about any given situation.

We are describing a person with good emotional control and a stable sense of self. This development happens slowly, over time, within the context of an attuned relationship connection.

So attunement grows brains! And misattunement followed by attunement can be a "brain growing" experience, too.

So is this news all good? Do all experiences grow your brain in beneficial ways? No, unfortunately, they do not. There is one kind of experience that does not grow your brain. It actually "prunes" your brain of neural connections. This is the feeling of fear and terror that you experience when your safety and well-being are seriously threatened.

# Fear, Terror, Trauma, and Pruning the Brain

It seems that nature intends for humankind to live in harmony. Harmonious relationships, which we have described as "attuned," and even misattunement followed by attunement, promote healthy brain growth and development. But nature also allows for protection against serious harm and injury by building in protective responses to threats. Some of the fascinating details of these reponses and their long-lasting consequences are discussed in chapters 4 and 5. For now, it is important to realize that experiences of fear and terror do *not* promote healthy brain development. In fact, the opposite is true. While attunement creates more and more neural connections, experiences of fear and terror, or trauma, destroy these connections. The destruction of neural connections during traumatic experiences is called neural "pruning." Repeated traumatic experiences destroy the pathways for emotional control that I have described.

> *Those who are traumatized repeatedly often end up with serious disconnections between their own feelings, thoughts, and actions. The presence of an external threat and the absence of an attuned relationship create internal disharmony and confusion.*

This is the kind of severe confusion, disharmony, and fear that I saw in Kim the day she walked into my office speechless and staring at the floor. One glance at her was enough to tell me that she desperately needed attunement. But what a challenge, now that she was so terribly injured! My task was to create the feeling of a safe haven in my office and to attune to her.

Is it hard to attune to an adult who won't speak? Not really. Babies don't speak, but we attune to them. The difference is that we don't expect babies to speak. We communicate emotionally with them without even thinking about it or questioning it.

Kim and I attuned wordlessly over the course of about two or three years. Gradually, she gained the ability to speak about her life and talk about her feelings. You will read from her journal in chapter 3, "Attachment."

# Summary

The facts about neural development—and, more specifically, about the development of emotional health—are clear. No one can or does "go it alone"—at least, no one who is emotionally healthy goes it alone. Psychological health begins in infancy within the context of a relationship with an attuned caregiver. The attuned caregiver's consistent, caring, appropriate, and well-timed interactions begin to create within the baby's brain the building blocks for a solid sense of self. Emotional attunement and appropriate misattunement or reattunement with a child literally pattern the child's brain in ways that reflect these healthy relationship experiences. Trauma prunes healthy connections and can, in a sense, "reverse" healthy experiences that may be taking place between traumatic experiences. The neural "pruning" that takes place during traumatic experiences can create an internal sense of confusion and insecurity because the sufferer may begin to feel out of touch with his or her own internal life. You will find out what this is like by reading more from Kim's journal in chapter 3.

This chapter has addressed the question of how relationships affect your sense of self and your ability to identify your emotions, feel them, and express or control them. Chapter 3 will show that such experiences accumulate over time into "attachment patterns." The attachment patterns affect your potential for future relationships. As attachment patterns are repeated through the generations, they can literally stamp the past onto the present and even onto the future.

# Chapter 3

# Attachment

IN CHAPTER 2 YOU LEARNED THAT THE ATTENTION of an attuned caregiver shapes a child's nervous system in ways that lead to a positive sense of self and good emotional control in future life. You also learned that trauma "prunes" the nervous system and can lead to a sense of internal confusion, poor self-understanding, and poor emotional control. This chapter will explain why, when Kim was in treatment with me, the advice she was given to stop feeling so bad about herself didn't work. She was told by doctors, therapists, and friends alike to change her thoughts and "stop thinking so negatively" about herself. She disclosed to me that no matter how hard she tried, she couldn't stop. She said she wasn't even "thinking" so much as "feeling" like a terrible, rotten, worthless person. This feeling pervaded all of her experiences every minute of her day.

We will explore why and how Kim's feelings about herself became so negative and why telling Kim to "stop feeling that way" or to try to "think her way to happiness" would not work. Kim's efforts alone were not enough to heal her because her nervous system did not have good emotional control patterns formed in it. She needed positive relationship experiences to "grow her brain" in ways that would give her this emotional control and a more solid, positive sense of self.

*The good emotional experiences that lead to positive
self-image and good emotional health are
called experiences of attachment.*

Let's look at a passage about Kim's early years from her journal
and see if there may be some clues to her later troubles in life back
in her childhood years. She writes,

*I was born the seventh out of ten children, six boys and four girls.
Our ages are a year apart, give or take a few months. My mother
supported the family on a waitress salary since my father left when I
was seven years old. We were extremely poor. My earliest memories
are of not having enough food, sometimes no electricity, and sometimes we had a hose running from my aunt's house next door so we
could have water. We very rarely had any meat, except every once in
while we had ground beef. Our "meat" was chicken every Sunday. I
still do not like chicken.*

*My earliest memory is of being lost and afraid. I was five years old
and living with another family. We had lost another house. We moved
eleven times in nine years. I don't know where my family was living.
The woman I was living with walked me to school in the morning,
and I was to walk home in the afternoon, but I got lost. I was wan-
dering around town, crying, when two women pulled up and asked
me if had an Aunt Evelyn who lived in the neighborhood. I replied,
"Yes," and they took me to her house, but I was still crying. I remember the woman coming to get me and laughing and hugging me
when I cried.*

*I used to get real attached to the female teachers who were nice
and paid attention to me. I even accidentally called one of them*

*"Mom" once. I didn't understand this attachment. It felt wrong. I was torn between wanting more of their attention and being ashamed at receiving any attention. I knew if they got to know me they'd see the badness inside me. I think I was drawn to my female teachers because I never received that motherly love from my own mother. As a kid, when I'd see a child with their parent, I would imagine what it felt like to have a parent hug you or hold your hand. I don't recall any hugs from any of my family ever, and that feeling of being lost, afraid, and alone has never left me.*

# Attachment, the Unseen Bond

Kim says that while she was growing up she used to get "real attached to the female teachers who were nice and paid attention" to her. She says that she "even accidentally called one of them 'Mom.'" She also says, "I didn't understand this attachment." These are Kim's exact words from her journal. She insightfully says that when someone was "nice and paid attention" she would get "attached." That is exactly what happens developmentally between children and their caregivers when the caregivers give the niceness and attention that we have called "attunement" in the last chapter. This repeated pattern of relationship between a parent and a child gives the child an internal feeling of safety and security, a feeling that there is someone to go to when fear or anxiety is aroused. The scientific literature, like Kim, has labeled this phenomenon "attachment."

The British psychiatrist John Bowlby is credited with introducing the concept of "attachment" into the scientific literature on mental health. After serving as an army psychiatrist for five years during World War II, Bowlby concentrated on child and family psychiatry. What he learned about the experiences of children separated from their mothers and fathers in early life piqued his interest in the effects of parents on children. He learned that children who lost their caregivers often suffered severe psychological distress. Sometimes the distress was so severe that it led to physical illness and even death. Bowlby was fascinated with this observation and began to explore it.

In the late 1940s the World Health Organization asked Bowlby to contribute to a study of the mental health needs of homeless children. His now famous monograph entitled *Maternal Care and Mental Health* was published in 1951 and later reprinted in many languages around the world. In this report Bowlby "called attention to the acute distress of young children who find themselves separated from those they know and love, and made recommendations of how best to avoid, or at least mitigate, the short- and long-term effects."[2] His work in the study of attachment continued throughout his life. Among his many publications is the seminal work *Attachment and Loss,* which continues to be a readable and rich source of thought and insight into the central role that relationships play in psychological health.

In recent decades a large body of scientific research and theory has expanded upon Bowlby's ideas. The field currently recognizes four "attachment styles" that can stand up to scientific study. One style, the secure style, is associated with excellent mental health, positive self-image, and high self-esteem in later life. People with a secure attachment style form good relationships easily and are able to maintain those relationships over time. Two styles labeled "insecure" are associated with less-than-ideal psychological health. These two styles are both associated with high levels of anxiety and are labeled "anxious resistant" and "anxious avoidant" in the literature. The fourth style, the one Kim experienced, is associated with poor mental health, negative self-image, and low self-esteem in later life. People with this fourth style of attachment often have poor emotional control and difficulty with relationships. This last style is labeled "disorganized/disoriented" in the literature. Research has shown that about 80 percent of abused children have this fourth attachment style. We will be discussing the first and last styles at length in relationship to Kim's story. We will examine how and why these styles emerge, how they affect a developing personality, and how the styles are transmitted from one generation to the next. Let's begin by considering how attachment begins between a parent and child.

## How Attachment Begins

Let's go back to your first days on the planet—only this time, instead of being the adult talking to the baby, you yourself are the baby. So, how are you, Baby? "Clueless," you would say if you could. "Totally clueless." If you could talk or think, which you can't, you would say, "I don't know who I am, I don't know who you are or who all these people are. I don't have any idea how to take care of myself. I am just a little innocent baby sitting here, looking at you."

So what did you do during that first few days? You did the only thing you could do. You attuned with your mom or another caretaker, and you just *were*. We talked a lot in chapter 2 about your first interactions with your mom (and I will use Mom as the example for the sake of convenience) and about how she attuned to you. She talked to you in eye-to-eye, face-to-face interactions that literally began to program your brain. You felt the pleasure of seeing her smiling face, and when it got too intense for you, you would look away. She would pause, too, ready to play the game again whenever you were ready. You and your mom were attuned. As time went on, she got even better at attuning with you. She learned how to "read you" and anticipate your needs, and she always seemed happy to be with you.

As time passed, you became used to Mom, and you liked that feeling of familiarity. You would look for her, and after only a few weeks you were able to distinguish her from others. You developed some expectations about her face, too. You came to expect that it would give you the pleasant feelings that no other faces gave you. So your brain "grew around" this experience, and you began to form an attachment to your mother. You recognized her, sought her attention, paid attention to her, and interacted with her whenever you could. This gave you pleasant feelings inside (if all was going well). Inside you, the bundling up of all of these experiences over time became your emotional attachment to your mother.

# Nature and Nurture in Action

*Attachment is a good example of the combination*
*of nature and nurture in action.*

Scientists say that we have the drive to form an attachment to our caregiver from the moment we are born. They say we don't have to develop this need because it is already there. That is our genes, or inherited nature, at work. This drive needs to be present at the moment of birth because it is crucial to our survival.

This same immediate bonding can be observed in the animal kingdom. From the first moments of life, mammals that are born alive and well immediately recognize their mother and know how to distinguish her from the other animals. You may have seen this phenomenon if you have ever been on a farm. You may have seen mother ducks with their young marching behind them down to the pond, or young colts teetering beside their mothers out in the pasture. In fact, so many animals form this bond of attachment that we take it for granted. How many times have you driven past a farm in early spring and seen the young calves standing next to their mothers? Have you ever wondered how the calves know their own mother? Have you ever wondered if the mothers have to sort out their young at the end of a day? And what about those amazing baby ducks parading like little soldiers behind their proud, waddling mom? Do they ever wander off and follow a lawn mower or a bulldog instead? No. In those first moments after birth, animals enter a critical period for attachment. They bond immediately to their mother, and this bond registers in their mind and body and remains. This bond has extremely high survival value. The mother protects her young during their formative period until this close proximity is no longer needed.

# The Wolf Girls

One of the more fascinating accounts of attachment and bonding is the story of the so-called "wolf girls." In a book titled *The Tree of Knowledge: The Biological Roots of Human Understanding,* biologists Humberto Maturana and Francisco Varela tell the story of two girls, ages five and eight, who were found in India in 1922 and had been raised by wolves. The authors report,

> At the time they were found, the girls did not know how to walk on two feet. They moved about rapidly on all fours. Of course, they did not speak and had inexpressive faces. They wanted only raw meat and exhibited nocturnal habits. They rejected human contact and preferred the company of dogs or wolves. At the time they were found, they were in perfect health and showed no signs of mental retardation or malnutrition. *Their separation from the wolf family caused a profound depression in them and brought them to the brink of death.*[3] [emphasis added]

Shortly after their separation from the wolves, one of the girls died, and although the other lived about ten years, she never gained fluent speech or developed social skills. She learned to walk on two feet, and ate with a knife, fork, and spoon, but she reverted to all fours under stress.[4]

Isn't that incredible? The little girls became attached to the wolf family and "grew around" this experience. They were used to living among wolves and had adjusted to that life. They didn't know anything else. When they were suddenly uprooted from their family and brought to "civilization," one of them died and the other nearly died as well. This really makes you think, doesn't it? It is an extreme case, and yet the same principles apply to everyone.

*You grow your brain around your experience, and this becomes part and parcel of who you are.*

And although the researchers were struck by the fact that the surviving girl never seemed to be completely human, it is impressive that she did gain some speech, even if it was not fluent, learned to walk on two feet, not four, and ate with utensils instead of eating the way the wolves do. She grew new ways of being, but her early attachments formed the bedrock of her personality. Why would this be?

## Attachment through the Generations

If we go back to chapter 2 and think about attuning with baby Matthew, we will remember that while you were attuning with him he was "borrowing" your emotional control system and sort of stamping it onto his emotional system. We said that this stamp, or relationship template, would form a part of the neural networks in his brain that would ultimately give him control over his emotions. It is as if Matthew were saying, "Hey, I don't have any emotional control yet, so I am going to borrow yours for a time while mine is growing. I am going to grow my emotional control to be just like yours, by the way. Well, what choice do I have, really? It is the only emotional control system I know about or *can* know about right now." And Matthew would be telling the truth.

Just like the little wolf girls, no baby in the world can decide that his parents are not fit to form a brain around, no matter how eccentric they may be! No baby can say, "Hey, these folks are a little too goofy for me. I can't handle this fur and tail thing. I think I will just go find someone else and stamp a template or two with some really together folks." No, you get what you get in the old parent-and-child match-up game.

So baby Matthew is going to get an emotional control system every bit as good or every bit as bad as the one his parents have come to rely upon. Just like the wolf girls, he is going to adapt his way of being, his brain, his personality, and his sense of self to the people who are helping him survive during these first years.

That's the good news and the bad news. It's good news for the child with a really together parent who passes on the "right stuff," and it's bad news for a child whose parent doesn't have the "right stuff" to pass on. In a moment we'll take a look at how this works by stepping into the research laboratory with the scientists who have discovered so much about how relationships change your brain.

## Observing a Relationship

I've described the importance of a parent's attuning to their child and argued that this attunement forms the healthy emotional pathways in the nervous system that eventually lead to good emotional control, positive self-esteem, and the ability to form close relationships with others. If this is true—and it is—then we would have to imagine that Kim's relationship with her mother was not well-attuned from the beginning of her life. We know that there were ten children in her family and that she was number seven. Wouldn't it be interesting if we could go back in time and watch Kim interacting with her mother? What do you think we would see?

Although we can't go back in time, we can make a pretty good guess about how Kim interacted with her mother by basing our hypothesis on the work of an amazing child development researcher named Mary Ainsworth. She became interested in studying not just children, but also their relationships with their mothers. She devised a clever research design called the "strange situation." In "strange situation" research, a child about one year old sits in an observation room with her mother and a bunch of toys. Then a number of experimental strange situations are created, and observers watch through a one-way mirror to see how the baby reacts as the situations change. Each different situation lasts about three minutes.

In one of Ainsworth's first studies, as described by John Bowlby in his book *Attachment,* mothers and babies were placed in a room with toys and were watched through the one-way mirror. During the first three minutes of the experiment, when the infants were alone with the mothers, most of them spent their time exploring the room, playing with the toys, and keeping an eye on their mother. Then, in the second segment, the researchers asked someone the baby did not know to enter the room with the baby and mother. When the new person entered the room, most of the babies explored the room a little less, but no radical changes took place in their behavior. Few, if any, of the babies cried at all during these first two scenarios. However, in the third segment, the mother left the room while the infant remained in the room with the stranger. Under this condition about half of the babies noticed that their mother was gone but remained calm, while the other half became distressed. Within the distressed group, there were further differences. Some babies became extremely upset, refused comfort from the stranger, and indicated that they wanted to be with their mother. A smaller group seemed to just give up and acted in a helpless manner.

You would think, based on all that we have discussed in the previous chapter, that all of the infants would be glad to see their mothers and would immediately go to them, seeking comfort and attunement to calm themselves when they returned. In fact, many of the babies did do this. But another group didn't react this way at all. In fact, they acted in a way that puzzled Ainsworth and those who read her early work.

Instead of greeting their mothers warmly, some of the infants ignored them completely, while others remained distressed and threw tantrums without actually trying to reach their mothers. Surprising results like these spurred a whole generation of research on attachment that continues to this day.

Although we can't actually go back in time and see for ourselves this pattern developing in Kim, we can imagine it. Let's just imagine we can look through Mary Ainsworth's window and see Kim interacting with her mother in a disorganized/disoriented style. I'll base my description on some of the scientific literature that describes this pattern. Imagine one-year-old Kim and her mother entering the observation room as we watch through a one-way mirror.

We see Kim and her mother enter the room. Kim sits in the room, about halfway between her mother and the toys. She looks very tentative and unsure of what to do. Her attention is drawn to the toys, and she goes to them and plays while keeping a watchful eye on her mother. When her mother leaves the room the first time, Kim becomes very upset, cries, and goes to the door. She can no longer play with the toys. When her mother comes back into the room, she sees her mother, continues to cry, and begins to move toward her. However, on her way there Kim stumbles and falls, even though nothing is in her way. She becomes even more upset now, and tries to get up to go to her mother. Suddenly, in the process of getting up, she freezes for about five seconds and remains motionless, as if frozen. Then she again tries to get up and go but appears to be moving in slow motion. Finally, as she reaches her mother, she again stops and looks dazed for a second until she crawls into her mother's lap, where she immediately arches her back and leans away from her mother while gazing at the floor and crying.

This is the disorganized/disoriented style of attachment. And for Kim, the feelings that began in infancy had not gone away by the time we met, which was well into Kim's adulthood. Here is what she said in one of her journal entries about meeting me for the first time:

*When I think about her I get afraid. My heart beats real hard and stuff. Why would she want to help me? She said I don't have to be afraid with her. Sometimes I want to be there and not be afraid, but I'm still afraid. Sometimes I think I like to see her even when I'm afraid. I don't get it. She's making me all confused.*

The "her" Kim is referring to is me, her therapist. But it would also fit pretty well for how she seemed to be feeling about her mother as we looked at her through the imaginary observation window, wouldn't it?

To be afraid of the person you need to turn to for protection is not how you are supposed to feel. Feeling drawn to someone while at the same time feeling as if you want to run away from that person is an unsolvable problem. To fear the one who is supposed to protect you is terribly confusing. And we can see it in Kim's behavior as we watch through the window. She seems to begin to move toward her mother, then she stumbles and falls. When she eventually crawls into her mother's lap, Kim arches her back as if to get away. These contradictory behaviors are outward expressions of her inner confusion. She becomes "disoriented," meaning she cannot take meaningful, purposeful action because she is trying to do opposite things at the same time.

Now, if we were to drive through the countryside and see a duckling acting this way—trying to move toward the mother duck, then rolling away on the ground, staggering toward her, then trying to bite her leg—we would immediately know there was something wrong, wouldn't we? Somehow, it just doesn't seem quite as obvious to us with people.

Let's look through the research window again, and this time, we'll watch a mother and child interacting in a secure attachment style. You got a pretty good picture of what to expect in chapter 2 when we talked about attunement. We are going to see something very different than what we observed with Kim and her mother.

## Secure Attachment

Let's imagine the mother is a friend of ours, and we are watching her and her child through the observation window. What would we see this time? Let's call this child "Teddy." Teddy and his mother enter the room. Teddy is immediately curious about the toys. He goes over to them and begins playing with them. When his mother leaves the room, he looks up and notices but goes back to his play.

When she comes back, he smiles and holds up the toy he is playing with and tries to reach out for her. She bends over and gets on his level. They begin to gaze at each other, eye to eye. She is picking up his excitement about the new toy, and she is getting into that flow with him.

"Oh, look at that!" she says in an interested voice. Now she sits on the floor, and they begin interacting gently with the toy. Later, she leaves again. Teddy looks a bit distressed this time and tries to move in the direction of the door. He seems to be waiting for her to come back and makes some crying sounds, as if to get her attention. When she reenters the room, he immediately goes to her. They hug for a minute or two, then he pulls away again, wanting to return to the toys.

It is easy to contrast the behavior of the two different styles. In the secure style, the child is obviously connected to his mother and is somewhat distressed by her absence. But when she is around, he is able to use her presence to give him a sense of comfort and courage that allows him to explore the new toys. He is so relaxed and interested in the toys that when she leaves for the first time, he is not concerned. He goes on playing. When she returns—and he seems confident that she will—he shows her the toys and wants to engage her in play. He is enjoying this and becomes disturbed by her leaving a second time. He is not afraid to tell her so! He makes some crying sounds. Now he is upset emotionally, so that when she returns, he needs a hug to calm down. He gets the hug he needs, regains his emotional balance, and goes back to playing.

In more scientific terms, we would say that when the mother left the room the second time, Teddy became "stressed" or "distressed." His emotional system signaled an alarm. When his mother returned, their attunement calmed and comforted him, as we discussed in chapter 2. The attunement allowed him to return to the secure feeling he had before he became distressed.

Notice, too, that Teddy was able to predict his mother's behavior and count on her reactions to meet his needs. He was so sure of her return to the room that he did not even react when she left the first time. He knew that he could get upset and receive comfort, and he did.

Unfortunately, Kim did not have a secure attachment style. But why not? Why was Kim's mother so scary to Kim? Why didn't Kim's mother attune, protect, pay attention, and care?

## Relationships through the Generations

Although Kim could not answer these questions, we can deduce the answers by looking at the findings of a group of researchers who followed up on Ainsworth's work. Developmental researchers Mary Main and Judith Solomon devised a research method in which the parents of the children watched through the observation window were interviewed about their own childhood experiences with relationships. The fascinating results showed a strong correlation between the parents' childhood experiences and the way they themselves parented their children. Parents who had had emotionally attuned caregivers were more likely to create secure attachment styles in their children. Parents who were either still overly emotionally involved with their own parents or were overly dismissive of the importance of family relationships tended to create insecure attachment styles in their children.

When these mothers were asked to tell their own stories of growing up, they responded in ways that made it obvious to the researchers that they still carried the scars of childhood traumas. Their responses were filled with gaps and holes and often failed to make a complete story that made sense. At times these traumatized parents would become so upset in the process of telling their own stories that they cried or had to stop the story altogether because recalling the painful events was simply too much for them. Sometimes as these mothers told their own stories of war, abuse, neglect, or abandonment they, like baby Kim, became frozen, confused, and disoriented.

So we see that the bonding of eye-to-eye, face-to-face attunement can pass on neural templates that create a sense of safety and comfort, or, as we see with Kim, the same process can pass on unresolved fear, terror, and sadness. This is why I always emphasize to parents how important it is that they become as emotionally healthy and strong as possible for the sake of their children. Trying to cover up old pain with a false face just doesn't work. The neural templates from trauma are there, and they operate whether we want them to or not.

*Denial can take the old pain out of consciousness for a while, but it doesn't destroy or eliminate it. It just buries it where it can do more harm than ever because it is now operating out of sight, outside of your awareness.*

# Summary

In this chapter we have seen how early relationship experiences with caregivers become organized into more complex patterns of relationship called attachment patterns. We have seen that the process of forming a bond with a caregiver is not conscious, and it is not done by choice. We, like the colts, calves, and ducklings, are programmed by nature to form a tight bond with our caregiver that helps to ensure our survival. We have seen that through the subtle and often overlooked dance of relationship between mother and child, the child's sense of himself or herself in the world is set down. The glance of reassurance, the outstretched arms of welcome, the attuned attention of the mother or father tell the child that the world is a safe and predictable place and that we are welcome in it. The distracted, preoccupied, and unpredictably harsh or frightening behavior of the mother or father with unresolved trauma and loss tells the child that the world is an unsafe and frightening place. It tells the child that although the caregivers are there to protect, that protection may or may not be there when it is needed. This uncertainty and lack of consistency create within the child a deep sense of insecurity and fear of the world. The child becomes confused about how to proceed. When is it safe to explore the world and when is it not? Will Mother or Father be here for me when I need them? How can I survive if they are not? And even more deeply the question is raised, What is it about me that makes my parents behave this way? What is wrong with me? In Kim's words, a feeling of being "made wrong" becomes lodged deep inside. An expectation builds that we are not acceptable and that things in life will go badly because of it. Healing, as we will find out, involves participation in relationships and experiences that can change this core belief.

In chapter 4 you will learn that the process of forming neural templates occurs during stress and trauma just as it does during bonding and relationship experiences. In fact, all experience is potentially "brain changing." However, stressful experiences and traumatic experiences are especially important to understand because one makes you stronger while the other does not. Stress creates a sense of mastery and resilience while trauma can create scars that last a lifetime—or, as we have seen, many lifetimes—as unresolved traumatic experiences can be passed from one generation to the next.

# Chapter 4

# Stress, Trauma, and Memory

Ever since the terrorist attacks on the World Trade Center in New York on September 11, 2001, the word "trauma" has become part of the national vocabulary. While most of us have heard the word many times since then, many are still unclear about what the word really means. What is the distinction between "trauma" and just a really bad event? What is the difference between trauma and simple loss or grief? Why do some people seem to go through terrible incidents and recover quickly, while other people seem never to recover? What accounts for these differences? And, most important, when traumatic loss and injury do occur, leaving in their wake the scars of painful emotions and debilitating memories, how does one heal? What is necessary? What is the process? These questions are the subject of chapters 4 and 5.

In this chapter I will define psychological trauma. I will compare the process of creating memories of "normal" events versus traumatic events. Then I will discuss healing from what I call "simple trauma." By "simple" I mean a one-time traumatic event that occurs to a person with a secure attachment style who was mentally and emotionally healthy before the trauma occurred. In chapter 5, "Harnessing the Power of Relationship to Heal Emotional Pain," I will discuss "complex trauma" and the process for healing from it.

# All in Your Head

Victims of trauma are often admonished to "just get over it." They are told that no matter what may have happened to them, it is over, it is in the past, and they should "leave the past behind and move on." They are often told, "What's done is done. Why talk about it? Nothing can change the past." Sometimes they are even told that the problems they are having recovering from the trauma are "not real." The troubles are "all in their head." These admonishments indicate a lack of understanding about memory processes in general and about traumatic memory in particular. They also draw on the misleading historical distinction between the mental and the physical.

Chapters 1 through 3 make clear that this distinction between what is "in the head" versus what is "in the body" is false. It is a myth. We know that experience changes neural templates that become integrated into the body and mind and exert an influence over future experience. The power of this dynamic will become even more dramatically clear as we turn to a discussion of normal memory processing versus traumatic memory processing. While both processes operate according to similar principles, there are important differences. Normal memory processing creates neural templates that integrate themselves so seamlessly into already existing memory stores that one hardly distinguishes memory formation from everyday living.

*Traumatic memory formation occurs during periods of extremely intense emotion, and traumatic memories are often stored in neural circuits*

*that replay over and over again. This is the traumatic*
*memory that just won't go away, the memory that*
*refuses to be forgotten.*

## Life-Threatening or Just Impressive?

As we begin our discussion of stress and trauma,

*It is important to realize that stressful events can,*
*under the right circumstances, make us stronger.*

I am reminded of a woman whom I heard give a speech about her
adventures sailing around the world. Someone in the audience asked
her if she had ever had to sail through a hurricane. She replied that
she had, in fact, many times. The woman in the audience got wide-
eyed and asked, "How do you *do* that?" The speaker answered,

*"When facing a thirty-foot wave, it is important to*
*ask yourself this question: Is this wave life-threatening,*
*or is it just impressive?"*

Life-threatening or just impressive. "Impressive" life events often
make us stronger. They can even be fun. Race-car driving and amuse-
ment parks depend on the fact that humans will choose stressful
events for fun. Notice the word "choose." And remember, the relative severity of a storm depends not only on the weather, but also
on the sailor. My circumnavigating heroine had seen many an im-

pressive wave in her day. It took a lot of storm for her to feel that her life was in danger. I am pretty sure that, although I am a sailor, had I been on the boat with her during one of her "impressive" storms, I may have evaluated the severity of the storm and the imminent risk to my life very differently than she did.

So what does this tell us? It tells us that when we evaluate any life event, many factors come into play. Some of the factors are external—such as the severity and duration of the event. (How big is the storm? How long will it last?) Other factors are internal—such as the ability to handle the event and remain safe. Our history plays a big role, too. (How skilled am I as a sailor? How much sailing experience do I have?)

My heroine had grown up with sailboats, raced them in college, and lived aboard boats for many years before she began her heroic solo journeys around the world. I had floated paper sail crafts down a stream behind my house, read lots of sailing adventure stories, and then bought a boat. Many of my heroine's waves would have been more than impressive to me if I had been in her shoes. Why? Because her brain had grown around the experience of sailing while mine had not. We cannot fully appreciate another person's experience from the perspective of our own life experiences. We cannot even fully appreciate our *own* childhood experiences from the perspective of adulthood.

When I met Kim, she didn't understand this concept. Her understanding of herself and her worthiness were based on all of the traumatic experiences she had endured. But she didn't say to herself, "Gee, I feel sort of bad about myself because I have so many emotional injuries and scars." No, she blamed herself. Here is what she had to say about this in her own words:

*I knew I must have been born wrong,*
*and that's why I deserved all of this.*
*There was something bad inside me.*
*I sometimes thought I was invisible,*
*or maybe I wished I was.*

*That way no one could look at me and see inside. See how disgusting*
*I was. Just having someone look at me made me shake sometimes. I*
*remember vividly the day my oldest brother brought home his girl-*
*friend. I came out of my bedroom to get a glass of water, and she*
*saw me and said, "Hi." I just froze, panicked, and went back to my*
*room, forgetting about the water. That's how I always felt, scared to*
*death. I was scared to be noticed. I was ashamed of being me. I used*
*to lie in my bed at night and cry to God, "Why do I have to be here?*
*Why can't you just let me die? What did I do so wrong to deserve*
*this?" Then I'd wake up the next day, disappointed that I was still*
*alive, and go through the motions again. I had no life.*

## Stress versus Trauma

Notice how many times within Kim's last, very short entry she uses
words that denote fear and terror. She says she used to "shake" whenever someone looked at her. She sometimes "froze" and panicked.
She often felt "scared to death." And in the same short entry she
talks about her own image of herself as "bad" and "disgusting" and
says she was "ashamed" of being herself. So we see here that the idea

we have been talking about so far—that relationships in great measure determine how we see ourselves—is evident in her writings. But Kim herself did not make this connection. Remember, the process of attunement creates neural templates during an unconscious process. The attachment process, too, is unconscious. The growth of the self-image, which is so closely tied to how we are loved and cared for by others, does not *seem to be* based on that. I will discuss this process, which is called "attribution," in greater detail in chapter 6.

Kim knew that her life had been difficult, even "stressful." But she did not understand that the experiences she had lived through were responsible for the terrible way she felt about herself. She didn't get the connection. She kept saying to herself, as others had suggested to her, "I need to get *myself* together." Although she had the intention and had even tried lots of different ways to help herself, she was trapped. Try as she might, she could not get her emotions and her behavior under control.

Perhaps that is one of the most important distinctions to make between the results of trauma and the results of stress. When you are under stress, you feel the stress, but when the stressor is removed, you feel better. You are able to "get yourself together" and carry on with your life, much the same as before.

*When you have suffered a traumatic injury,*
*that injury can seem to take*
*on a life of its own.*

# Disclaimer

The study of trauma has blossomed into a whole new field of scientific inquiry now officially called psychotraumatology. The number of studies of the biochemical processes associated with memory, stress, and trauma is overwhelming, and their complexity is daunting. Almost daily, new discoveries are challenging our old ideas of what trauma is all about.

The information I am about to present is a distillation of some of the current understanding in the field. It is by no means detailed or complete. I urge interested readers to refer to the books and journal articles listed at the end of this book to gain a more thorough understanding. I have decided to err in the direction of simplicity to avoid overwhelming the reader with too much complexity for the sake of accuracy. The information presented here has been chosen for its relevance to the experience of healing from trauma. I will refer to only two of the many parts of the brain's anatomy that are involved in trauma and will greatly simplify the chemical processes that are involved when the experiences of memory, stress, and trauma play themselves out in our everyday lives.

# How Memory Happens

I am going to discuss two areas in the anatomy of the brain. Both are in the middle of the brain and are a part of a number of structures that operate together and form what scientists call the limbic system. The first structure within the limbic system that I want to mention is the amygdala.

*The amygdala is the emotional relay center*
*of the brain.*

It receives sensory information, helps focus attention, and then sends the information along to another area in the brain called the hippocampus.

*The hippocampus is the memory relay center*
*of the brain.*

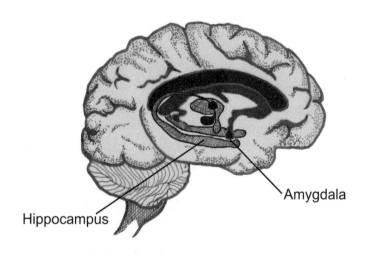

Fig. 6
The Limbic System

It puts the information in sequence over time. Then the information is relayed to the higher centers of the brain to become part of long-term memory. Within the flow of this process, the new incoming information is also compared to old information from stored memory and evaluated in terms of whether or not this new event is significant.

Let me give an example of how this works. Suppose I am on my thirty-five foot sailboat, all by myself in the middle of the Chesapeake Bay. I am feeling the sun on my face, feeling the boat swaying back and forth, and experiencing a feeling of happiness. This happy-feeling information is going to my amygdala, the emotional relay center. The amygdala is "reading" the emotion and sending signals to other parts of my brain and body, based on this reading. "She is OK," says the emotional relay center. "She is feeling safe and happy. All is well." Then the hippocampus (along with many other places in the brain) receives the messages from the emotional relay center and starts storing happy memories of sailing in my brain's memory networks.

Later on, if you ask me to tell you my sailing story, I will be able to do that because the emotional relay center and the memory relay center in my brain have done their jobs. They have taken my sailing experiences, "colored" them with emotion, sequenced and ordered them in time, and sent them to my memory storage centers. When I want to, I can tell sailing stories that are in logical historical sequence. These stories will make sense and will bring me happy feelings as I tell them. This is the way things go when memory storage is what I will label "normal."

# Mild Stress and Normal Memory Storage

Now let us suppose I am sailing and see a storm coming up, far off in the distance. Now what will happen?

Now I shift gears emotionally. My emotional relay center is getting a different message. Instead of contentment and relaxation, the new emotion I feel is fear. I am perceiving a threat to my safety. The emotional relay center sends an alert signal to the chemical centers of the brain to shift gears. The "all is well" signal to the amygdala will now be instantaneously replaced with the alert signal that is designed to mobilize my body and mind in ways that protect me from harm.

"Alert!" says the emotional relay center. "Possible threat on the horizon!" This internal alert signal will cause my attention to narrow and focus on the perceived threat.

Now let us imagine I realize that the black cloud I see is coming from a factory that is far from shore and is not part of a storm front. Ah, I can relax. My fear dissipates, and my attention again diffuses to the pleasant day and the feelings of boating. This experience is being recorded as it happens by the memory relay center in my brain. This memory storage process is very sensitive to the amount of emotion that comes in with the memory information. In general, as described in chapter 2, more intense emotion leads to more vivid memory. The neural templates that form in response to an event are more permanent if that event was experienced under conditions of intense emotion. In the future I will retain a memory of this "black cloud" experience, but it is not likely to be very vivid. This whole event lasted only a second or two and did not generate intense emotion. It was, in the language of a scientific textbook, a "mild stressor." In everyday language we would say, "It turned out to be nothing."

Notice a number of things here. Notice that sensitivity to my emotion of fear immediately generated a total-body response designed to assess danger and protect me. Notice also that while the danger remained, my body's internal resources were mobilizing to deal with it, but when the danger passed and a feeling of safety was reestablished, my body, mind, and emotions returned to a calm state.

# Terror to Triumph and Vivid Memory Storage

Now let us suppose that I sail along a little farther and the wind dies down. My boat comes to a halt right in the middle of a narrow shipping channel. I go into the alert state described above and immediately attempt to start my engine so that I can get out of the way of a huge shipping vessel I can see coming right at me in the distance. It will crash into me if I stay here in the narrow channel. These huge, lumbering tankers take over a mile to make a turn and barely fit in the channel. If my boat remains where it is, I know I will be hit in less than fifteen minutes. I scramble to start my engine to move out of harm's way. The engine will not start. It won't even turn over. I am stuck! No motor, no wind. Now what? Now my emotional relay center is getting a strong alarm! Fear has turned to terror as I perceive my situation is potentially life threatening. The chemicals being released now include adrenaline and other substances that increase my ability to perform under pressure.

My heart rate is increasing, and more blood is being pumped into my muscles so that I can be strong and quick. I am breathing hard. This is the physiological "fight-or-flight" response we get in response to life-threatening danger. My thoughts seem to be racing through my options—jump overboard and swim (no, too slow) or call for help (no one around). I am beginning to feel panicky. Suddenly, a stiff breeze begins to blow from the east. With lightening speed and accuracy, I arrange the sails to catch the freshening breeze. I am carried smoothly away from the path of the oncoming tanker. I breathe a sigh of relief! My terror fades to relief and gratitude. The emotional information from my emotional relay center signals that the threat is passed. A feeling of safety and rest returns.

The hippocampus has recorded this event very vividly.

*The high level of emotional intensity coupled with the potential threat to my safety mean that the memory will be strong and not easily dismissed or forgotten.*

You can be sure that I will avoid the shipping channels on my next expedition! Still, this will make a very good story. My hippocampus has done its job. It relayed this intense experience in sequence to my long-term memory stores. My story has all the elements of a tale I will want to tell often—a challenge to safety, the action of escape, and a happy ending. The lasting feeling is one of triumph over adversity.

This kind of experience can often leave one feeling exhilarated and can raise self-esteem higher than it was before the experience. Those who engage in "extreme sports" such as mountain climbing and NASCAR racing know this. Such athletes will talk about the "adrenaline rush" and the feeling of exhilaration they get when they purposely face a life-threatening situation. They choose this experience and feel prepared to handle it because they are confident that the threat sequence—fear, then flight or fight—will have the happy ending of safety and triumph.

Even if the athletes don't win their events,

*Moving through experiences that cause fear and emerging from them with a sense of mastery is beneficial because it strengthens one's ability to handle similar stress in the future.*

This is because early in the fear-producing sequence, as you assess the threat, you will recall similar threats from which you emerged successfully. You also will have formed templates in your mind that begin to handle this type of stress as "routine." You have a tendency to remain coolheaded and not to let your emotions rage out of control. In physiological terms, you don't flood your amygdala with emotion, because your previous experiences have taught you how to behave, how to move your body through this experience, and how to keep a balance between your emotions, sensations, and thoughts.

The movements your body makes during these times of athletic stress will be crucial. If you've ever seen skiers at the top of a hill before a race, you have probably noticed them bobbing up and down, shaking off the jitters. Golfers, before they hit the ball, often shake their clubs and wiggle their bodies around to loosen up. (My dad used to call it "the waggle.") Many of us have seen or experienced these sensations ourselves—the connection between body movement and getting control over rising levels of tension and stress. These body movements, coupled with successful experiences of having moved through similar stress in the past, coupled with a feeling of choosing this to happen because of confidence in a positive outcome, all combine to make skiing, sailing, and tournament golf fun experiences.

Now let us turn to the issue of other kinds of life experiences that also involve the fear cycle but do not have a happy ending. These we will label "trauma."

# Terror without Triumph—Traumatic Memory Processing

Let's turn again to Kim to learn about just one of her many traumatic experiences. We will distinguish between the stress described in my boating experience and the trauma that Kim endured. Then we'll look at the brain processes that occur during trauma and see how they differ from the stress responses I have described.

Kim writes,

> *At nights when I was around eleven years old, one of my oldest brothers would come to my room to get me. I would wake up as soon as I heard his footsteps on the floor outside my room. I would immediately become terrified, and I would freeze up and hide under my covers, as if I were hoping he wouldn't see me, as if I were trying to be invisible. He would take me into his room to have sex. With him. I can still see it as if I'm watching it happen to someone else. We both*

*have our shirts on, but not our pants. He is lying on top of me. I can see the pain on my face, my hands next to me, squeezing the sheets. I was so afraid, and I had no one to help me.* **The feelings were so intense that when I thought I could bear it no more, everything changed. It was as if things were moving in extremely slow motion and I began to feel numb. Eventually my hands relaxed and I just felt like I was limp. It was better than the pain. It was like I was floating in the air, watching it from the ceiling.**\* *Afterward he would give me something that belonged to him. Payment to his whore. . . . I don't remember fighting or saying "No." Why?*

*Kim's description of her traumatic experience is much different than my encounter with the tanker in the bay.*

When the tanker was bearing down on me I was anything but "limp" or "numb" and moving in "slow motion." My thoughts were racing to find a way to save myself—to get away or fight back. Kim asks why her experience with her brother was not more like my run-in with the tanker. Why, she asks, did she not fight or say "No"? As she writes and remembers her lack of action, she makes a judgment against herself. She blames herself for "allowing" the abuse to happen. Even from the adult perspective from which she now writes, she can find no reason for her passivity, her lack of resistance. And so she condemns herself. She says she is her brother's "whore."

---

\* Emphasis added.

**Stress or Trauma?**

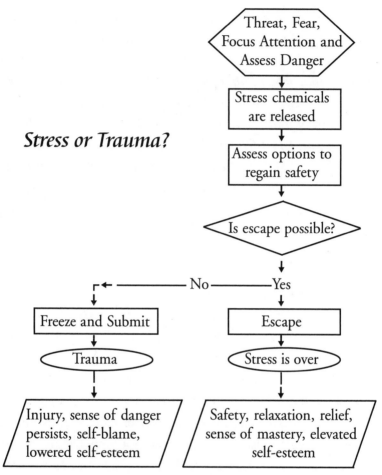

Fig. 7
Stress versus Trauma

Let's take a look at the diagram in Figure 7 and compare my experience to the trauma that Kim endured.

Notice that both scenarios begin with a perceived threat and fear. In both situations, attention is focused, danger is assessed, stress chemicals are released, and options for regaining safety are assessed.

But in the trauma experience, freezing and submission take the place of the movement of running away or fighting. Why?

*It is the fact that escape is not possible that makes Kim's experience very different from mine.*

Let's return to the brain to see what happens to Kim during her brother's attack that differs from what was going on inside my brain during the tanker experience on the bay. Kim and I both have our brain's emotional relay center—the amygdala—at rest when the two sequences begin. I am happily sailing, Kim is sleeping in bed. Suddenly, both of us are thrust into a state of fear. Kim hears her brother's footsteps, and I see the tanker on the horizon. Inside both of our brains, chemicals are being released to help us protect ourselves from danger. Both of us make an assessment: Is escape possible? I am on the bay, thinking of jumping overboard and calling for help. Kim is lying in her bed. I am running about the boat like crazy, trying to start the engine, working with the sails to try to catch a breeze. I obviously believe that I can escape if I take the right action. My body is receiving lots of extra help from the chemical changes that are taking place in my body and in my brain as I face this threat. I am getting more blood to my muscles, I am breathing harder. Obviously, I am expecting to move out of harm's way.

When Kim feels the threat, she goes into a state of hypervigilance. In other words, her attention narrows and focuses on the incoming threat, just like mine did when the tanker was coming at me. But when Kim makes her assessment, she realizes that she can neither run nor fight. This assessment is based on having already been abused for years, on her young age and lack of strength compared to her brother, and on her lack of protective support from anyone else in the family. She is unable to fight, there is nowhere to flee to, and no one will help her.

> *Escape is not possible. Kim's emotional relay center reacts to this realization with a higher level of arousal, one that puts her "over the edge" and triggers the body's last-ditch defensive posture—the freeze response.*

Kim becomes motionless, goes "numb," and hides under the covers. She describes it as "trying to be invisible" or trying to "disappear." Another way of describing the situation is to say she is trying to escape her predator's notice.

According to psychologist Peter Levine, this response is very similar to the response of an animal in the wild that is overcome by a predator. According to Dr. Levine, the purpose of the freeze response is to numb the pain of imminent injury or death. In his book *Waking the Tiger—Healing Trauma,* Dr. Levine discusses the freeze response, quoting David Livingstone, the missionary and explorer who wrote of his own life-threatening encounter with a lion in Africa. Livingstone compared this numb state to the "'stupor . . . felt by a mouse after the first shake of the cat.'" He wrote,

> "I heard a shout. Startled, in looking half round, I saw the lion just in the act of springing upon me. . . . he caught my shoulder as he sprang, and we both came to the ground below together. Growling horribly close to my ear, he shook me as a terrier does a rat. . . . It caused a sort of dreaminess in which there was no

sense of pain nor feeling of terror, though quite conscious of all that was happening. It was like what patients partially under the influence of chloroform describe, who see all the operation, but feel not the knife. This singular condition was not the result of any mental process. The shake annihilated fear, and allowed no sense of horror in looking round at the beast. This peculiar state is probably produced in all animals killed by the carnivore; and if so, is a merciful provision by our benevolent creator for lessening the pain of death."[5]

Dr. Levine labels the experience Livingstone describes as "dissociation." He writes, "Dissociation is one of the most classic and subtle symptoms of trauma . . . [It] seems to be a favored means of enabling a person to endure experiences that are at the moment beyond endurance—like being attacked by a lion, a rapist, an oncoming car, or a surgeon's knife."[6]

## From Numb to Pain and Back Again

In Kim's journal entry she describes an incident of sexual abuse in which she went "numb" and failed to fight against her assailant. We can say now that she "dissociated" during this experience. Unconscious, automatic defenses were activated in this life-threatening situation, enabling her to endure the experience without fully experiencing the pain and agony of it. Kim's journal makes it clear that abusive experiences were a common—in fact, daily—occurrence in her earlier life. We can guess that dissociating became a common defensive response for her. She used dissociation and substance abuse to numb herself to the daily onslaught of emotional pain in her life.

Living in this numb state of emotion is very uncomfortable.

*Think about how it feels to go to the dentist and have your mouth partially numbed. It's true that you don't feel any pain, but is the experience pleasurable?*

Aren't you anxious for the anesthesia to wear off so that you can feel something again? You want to feel, right? It is unpleasant, sort of eerie, and unsettling to feel even partially numb. Now think about what it would be like if your whole body were feeling this way. And think about feeling this way not merely for an hour or two, but for weeks at a time. I recently talked with a woman who said she had felt numb for her entire life. She could describe for me only one or two instances in which she actually felt her body and her emotions simultaneously and could remember the experience. She described the cool breeze on her cheek one summer day as she stared at a cherry tree in bloom. The experience lasted only a moment, but she remembered it. It stood out from the landscape of numbness that was her life.

Now read another section from Kim's journal as she explains that to try to "feel" things, she engaged in outrageous behaviors. She swam in freezing water and raced fast cars. She enjoyed these chosen adrenaline rushes because of two things. First, they gave her a momentary feeling of *something,* and second, they were potentially life threatening. She would have been happy to die to escape the pain of living. As she writes in her journal, her life "meant nothing" to her.

*I don't recall talking much as a kid. I didn't think I had anything to say worth listening to. I thought everything about me was stupid—my thoughts, my looks, my feelings—everything. My days were pretty much the same. I woke up, showered, and went to the school bus stop. There my brother (he was a year older than me) would begin his verbal assault. Then, on the bus, he would get most of the other kids to go along with him telling me how ugly I was and making fun of the fact that I didn't have any friends. Like I needed reminding. When we arrived at school, we weren't allowed to go right in. We had to wait on the playground for a little bit. I just sat on the porch and watched the other kids play. I didn't know how to join them, and I was sure they wouldn't want me near them anyway. I feel like my whole life I stood on the outside watching everyone else live. I didn't know how to be a participant.*

*Sometimes during the school day I would have to lay my head on my desk because I would start to cry. I was always so sad. I never felt good about myself. I would have to go to the nurse twice a day to drink milk and take medication for a stomach ulcer. My stomach hurt a lot. I had to have a special diet. I also had inner ear reconstructive surgery due to a birth defect. This resulted in a hearing loss. None of these things helped my popularity. Daily life was painful. I knew early on that I was different. It was painful to be around people and feel so apart. I didn't know who I was, how I fit, or how to be.*

*After school would be the long bus ride home to be assaulted some more. While most of the neighborhood kids went outside to play after school, I stayed in my room, hoping to be left alone. I didn't have any friends, so I had nowhere to go. For years I was rarely left alone. If my brother was home he would verbally assault me to the point that I tried to stab him on two separate occasions. Other times he and an-*

*other brother would bring their friends home. My brothers would sit and watch TV while their friends tormented me. One time when they were trying to get my clothes off, I got away before they could get my underclothes off. I ran outside in the snow and hid in an old junk car until they left. Another time I was told to put on boxing gloves, and they proceeded to hit me on the back of the head (they called them rabbit punches) until I almost passed out.*

*When I did leave the house it was usually to walk next door to see if my cousin was home. Often her older brother was home, and I'd have to play hide-and-seek. When he found me he got to have sex with me. And sometimes I would have to perform oral sex on him. I still remember the smell and the taste. Oh, how I tried to hide so well. I don't remember saying "No" or fighting. I'll never forget how disgusted I was with myself. I can still easily go there. I wish I could remember fighting him.*

*When I was still in grade school, I went snooping through my mother's room one day and found a whole drawer full of filled prescription bottles. When I got older I realized that some of the pills I had taken were vitamins, but some were pain pills. I took a handful and found that I didn't care anymore. I didn't care how I felt about myself or about anything. From that day on, my life changed. I began taking pills regularly and drinking, too, when I could get it.*

*During my fifteen-year addiction I did a lot of things that could have resulted in a shorter life span. In the neighborhood there was a lake where we used to go swimming. The lake would go over a dam and into a stream about one to two feet deep. The stream had stumps and bottles and trash in it. I used to let the current drag me over the dam to see how far I could safely make it down stream. I would go swimming in January so I could be the first swimmer of the year. I*

*fell through the ice on the lake twice one winter, and at age eighteen*
*I began legally drag racing professionally at some local drag strips. In*
*the five years I did that, I only lost one race. I loved the speed and the*
*fact that if I didn't slow down quickly enough I could run into the*
*woods. My life meant nothing to me.*

# No Memory, No Story, No "Me"

There were many reasons why Kim's life "meant nothing" to her.
First, she was in constant emotional pain from the ongoing trauma
in her home. Second, neither escape nor fighting back were possible, so she lived in a constant state of dissociation and numbness.
Third, the traumatic events disrupted her memory so severely that
she felt fragmented, confused, and disoriented inside. People with
chronic, repetitive trauma like Kim's complain that they "don't know
who they are." They remember only fragmented bits and pieces of
their personal story. Some of the trauma can remain isolated from
long-term memory, and older events become blurred and disrupted.
To understand this you must understand something about normal
memory and how it works. Then we will take a look at traumatic
memory to see the differences.

# Normal Memory

Normal memory, as I will call it, is a fascinating and complex process. Like many other brain processes we have already discussed,

what we know about memory is being challenged daily by new discoveries in brain science. Despite the controversies that arise as new information challenges old ideas, scientists have come to agree on some basic ideas about memory storage that are important for our understanding. The first key idea is that memory is not just memory. There are different kinds of memory storage systems.

*There is memory that is short-term, which is the kind you use to remember a phone number between the time you read it in the phone book and the time you dial it. Then there is long-term memory, the kind you use to remember your address for future reference.*

Long-term memory can be either conscious or unconscious, and it can be for actions and tasks as well as for information you have to remember. For instance, when it is time to get dressed, you need both conscious memory to tell you whether or not you are going to go to work today, and you need the unconscious motor programs that are stored in your long-term memory to guide you in tasks such as buttoning your shirt and tying your shoes.

In terms of our discussion, both long- and short-term memory create neural templates. However, the short-term templates deteriorate and fade unless the information they contain is transferred and incorporated into long-term memory. Long-term memories associate themselves together and, over time, create your "story." Like all the brain processing systems we have discussed, memory does not work like a machine. It is nothing like a video camera, a tape recorder, or a transcript. As new experience is integrated into the long-term memory stores, the information is organized and re-organized as necessary. New information is added, and old information may fade or be reinterpreted in terms of new experiences. Let's look at this process more closely.

# Blessed Forgetting

As you may recall from chapter 1, neural templates are constantly organizing and reorganizing. Old templates are destroyed while new templates are created and integrated into the patterns that account for our perceptions, our story, and our entire sense of self. Memory is selective, meaning that not all of the things you experience will be stored within your long-term memory. Certain things are stored and, therefore, remembered, and certain things are not. They are forgotten.

Forgetting has gotten a bad reputation in our culture. We tend to associate it with aging or disease. But

*Forgetting is a normal and extremely valuable part of the biology of the mind.*

Just think about it. What if you were burdened with the precise memory of every piece of minutia that you encounter every day of your life? What if you remembered the names and page numbers of your first-grade readers and the taste and texture of the food you ate when you were a baby? What if you could never forget the pain of childbirth or the shame of your most embarrassing moment? What if all of this information and more were crowded into your waking consciousness every moment of every day? You might say, "Well, I would go crazy. It would be too much." So forgetting is key.

I once worked with an amazing Irish woman who had a chronic illness that caused her to begin to lose her long-term memory. She had always been a bright, sassy woman with a razor sharp wit. As I saw her failing, I felt sorry for her. I said one day, "I am sorry that you are having such a hard time with your memory." "Ah, my dear," she answered, shaking her brilliant red hair and waving her hands in dismissal, "it is of no matter. There are so many things in life worth forgetting!"

## The Unfinished Novel of Your Life

So, in normal memory storage, what gets remembered and what gets forgotten? Three concepts are important here. First, in general, things that are crucial for your survival will be remembered. Second, experiences associated with high levels of emotion will be remembered. Third, all things being equal,

*The general memory of a big event will be*
*remembered while the smaller details of that*
*event will fade with time.*

For instance, it is amazing that we Americans can drive cars at high speeds so close together and have as few accidents as we do. Very seldom do any of us forget which side of the road to drive on. Very seldom do we forget the meaning of a red light or a green light. The idea that one could forget such things seems absurd. But in fact this is memory at work. This is unconscious memory with very high survival value. Forget, even for a moment, and it could cost you your life.

High emotion will make a big imprint on memory. For example, many of us vividly remember the day we got our first car. We remember because it was usually a day of high emotion—pride, excitement, perhaps even a little anxiety—as we ventured out into a new phase of life. But if I were to ask you what you were wearing that day (assuming it wasn't recent) you would probably not recall. This detail would be lost in the normal stores of your long-term memory, and this is how normal memory works. The occurrence of the big event will be integrated into your memory. Then the event will fade into the background of your consciousness until you choose to "call it up" from your long-term stores. As you recall it, it will reappear as a part of your story. As time goes on, the memory of the day you got your first car will remain a memory, but the meaning of that fact may change as your story evolves. For example, if you later become a race-car driver, the day you got your first car will take on enormous significance. Every detail of that day may become important to retain as you tell the story over and over. If not, the details may fade as other events in your life take on more importance.

The fact that memories change as the meaning of past events changes is illustrated by the oft-repeated "starving artist" story. After an actor achieves fame and fortune, he may tell of his days as an aspiring, undiscovered actor with fondness and warmth. Those days of slinging burgers in the greasy spoon will glow with nostalgia as he looks upon them as first steps on his road to stardom. If you could go back in time to ask this same man how he feels about actually being a poorly paid cook in an all-night diner, he probably would have a very different story to tell. "This stinks," he might say. "I hate this. I feel like a loser." Which is correct? Is the cook a loser or a budding star? It depends on when you ask him and what happens next.

*Memory is a storymaker. It, like all the other*
*aspects of the mind that we have discussed,*
*interacts with experience as it unfolds*
*and creates templates that guide*
*and inform your future.*

Memory, too, is alive and busy writing the unfinished novel of your life.

# Traumatic Memory

If memory is alive, then traumatic memory has a life of its own. It is different from normal memory. Traumatic memories, by definition, immediately create their own neural templates as the trauma occurs. Then these "freestanding" neural networks often do not get integrated into the long-term memory stores. Instead, they "sit," "freeze-dried" in their original form, ready for instant replay. And replay they do, without the consent of the owner.

*Traumatic memories are memories that refuse to be*
*forgotten. They repeat again and again in the form*
*of flashbacks, nightmares, and intrusive thoughts*
*and feelings about the traumatic event.*

They are often very resistant to change. They are one of the hallmarks of a psychological disorder that sometimes occurs in people who, like Kim, undergo a terrifying experience that causes long-lasting psychological problems.

# Post-Traumatic Stress Disorder

Post-traumatic stress disorder is the name given to an anxiety disorder that can come about as a result of extreme trauma. Not all people who experience extreme trauma will develop it, but many do. The trauma can take many forms, but it has generally been found to result either from experiencing, witnessing, or being confronted by actual or threatened death or serious physical injury, or a threat to the physical integrity of oneself or others.

*Though the causes of such extreme trauma can be various, the victim's immediate response to it is one of fear, helplessness, or horror.*

Physical assault, motor vehicle accidents, war and combat experiences, torture, brainwashing, and natural catastrophes such as earthquakes, hurricanes, tornadoes, and floods are all examples of the types of experiences that can lead one to develop post-traumatic stress disorder. Vicarious experiences of trauma—in other words, watching someone else being traumatized—can also lead to post-traumatic stress disorder.

The symptoms associated with post-traumatic stress disorder may not become evident immediately after the trauma, but when they do in the days, weeks, months, or even years after the event, they fall into three main clusters:

1. Reexperiencing or reliving the event through
    • recurring distressing and intrusive memories of the event
    • recurring distressing dreams of the event

- flashbacks in which it feels as if the event is actually happening again
- intense feelings of distress at any reminder of the event
- physical reactions such as chills, heart palpitations, or panic when faced with reminders of the event

2. Avoiding reminders of the event and emotional numbing
   - avoiding thoughts, feelings, or associated conversations
   - avoiding activities, places, or people that are reminders of the event
   - inability to recall an important aspect of the trauma
   - withdrawal from, or markedly less than usual interest in everyday activities
   - feelings of detachment or estrangement from others
   - a restricted range of emotion (feeling numb or "dead" inside); this often looks and feels like depression
   - a sense of a foreshortened future

3. Persistent symptoms of increased arousal, anxiety, or nervousness such as
   - a feeling of being on edge, waiting for the next bad thing to happen
   - difficulty falling or staying asleep
   - irritability or outbursts of anger
   - difficulty concentrating
   - being "jumpy" or easily startled

When post-traumatic stress disorder develops, the trauma survivor will begin to experience significant distress or impairment in his or her social life, employment, or other important areas of life.

# A Mugging and Post-Traumatic Stress Disorder

To see how post-traumatic stress disorder can develop, let's take a look at an example of a simple trauma and what can happen in its wake. By "simple trauma" I mean a trauma that occurs one time and stops.

Suppose you are walking down the street alone one day, and suddenly a pair of thugs in ski masks jumps out of a doorway and holds you at gunpoint. The first guy tells you to stop or he'll blow your brains out. The second guy demands your money and jewelry. You suddenly fear for your life. Panic-stricken, you wrench your ring from your finger, rip off your watch, and struggle to find your wallet. You shove your belongings into the hands of your assailants and stand in a state of frozen terror as the two thugs run off and disappear into an alley.

Based on our discussion so far, do you think you will have psychological difficulty after this incident? After all, physically, nothing has happened to you. The robbers did not even touch you. Let us also assume for our discussion that nothing like this has ever happened to you before and that you have a secure attachment style and a good support system. Will templates form in response to this event?

Yes. How could they not?

Will the templates be stored only briefly in short-term memory, move fluidly to long-term memory, fade out the details, and easily become a part of your story as I described? Well, maybe, but chances are, unless you are a person who already has had experience dealing with life-threatening events and this is just "another one of those," this incident is likely to leave a deep imprint that will not easily fade. Why? Because it is associated with survival and extremely high levels of emotion and because the intense fear you experienced may have overwhelmed your normal memory processing mechanisms. If you develop post-traumatic stress disorder, it will be because your mind had to rely on this built-in defensive response that protects it from overwhelming experience. Rather than mix this experience into normal memory stores, it reroutes it to its own neural pathways, where it remains separate and freestanding. This does two things: It protects the "rest" of you from the overwhelming emotion associated with this event, and it allows you to deal with the event later, after it is over.

Let's say this memory does not move naturally into long-term memory stores but instead becomes locked into its own neural pathway and you develop the symptoms of post-traumatic stress disorder. What would that be like? It would not be comfortable at all. You would reexperience the mugging over, and over, and over again as if it were happening for the first time. While this is happening, you would feel the same fear and terror that you felt during the original event. This reexperiencing—or "flashback," as it is commonly called—might happen to you when you are awake and doing other things, or it could happen when you are sleeping. You would find that you cannot control the onset of these flashbacks. After a few of these episodes, you would begin to notice that the likelihood of the trauma's replaying itself is greater when you are near the street where it happened. You would begin to try to avoid that street. You might also notice that you have a flashback when you watch television shows that depict robberies. You might stop watching shows like this. In other words, you would be continually reexperiencing the trauma and also trying to avoid anything that would trigger the flashbacks.

Unfortunately, you would find that post-traumatic stress disorder would begin to dominate more and more of your life because, despite your best efforts to avoid things that remind you of the mugging, you would continue to experience the event over and over again. You might notice that you could be at home, safe and snug on your own living room couch, when suddenly the event would replay. You wouldn't know why, but later you might realize that you heard a car door banging shut outside. The noise startled you. Your body reacted with a brief fear response in reaction to the startle. This brief instant of fear was enough to trigger the flashback.

Over time, external events that might be associated in some vague way with the original event and even internal "events"—such as thoughts, feelings, or body sensations—could trigger the replay. If this were to continue, your overall level of distress and daily anxiety would skyrocket. People I have treated for post-traumatic stress disorder have complained that they felt as if they were "losing their mind." The flashbacks are extremely painful. While they were happening, you would begin to shake with fear and tremble with panic. You would have an overwhelming urge to run or fight. As this is happening, you might have thoughts that you feel as if you are losing your mind because these feelings are so unbearable and unstoppable. At night you might be afraid to go to sleep because nightmares of the event could awaken you in a sweat of panic. You might sometimes scream out loud as you startle awake. Over and over, people would tell you that the event is in the past, but it won't feel as if it is in the past.

In fact, more and more things would trigger these flashbacks. You might find that you can't watch television anymore because the cop shows are a trigger. You may have trouble going out on the street to shop because the sidewalk is a trigger. You hate the sight of ski apparel. You assess every man you see on the street, wondering, "Could it have been him?" The event begins to dominate your life, your emotions, your thoughts. People are getting tired of seeing you deteriorate. They keep saying, "Nothing really happened. Who cares if you lost your ring and some money? You didn't get hurt. They never touched you." And so, after a time, you decide you need some help, and you come to see me. Your doctor has sent you because he has heard that I deal with "stress." What would I say?

# Treatment for Simple Post-Traumatic Stress Disorder

First, I would explain all the things about "normal" memory that we have just discussed in this chapter. I would then explain the kind of memory you have of the holdup. I will call it "traumatic memory." Traumatic memory is similar to normal memory in a couple of ways. First, it is recorded under conditions of high emotion, and, as with normal memory, the stronger the emotion, the stronger the memory. But remember, you feared for your life during the holdup.

*The fear you experienced was about as strong as strong can be. And so this holdup memory is "stamped" into your neural circuits.*

But unlike normal memory, this memory circuitry is not so plastic. Instead, it is rigidly contained in seeming isolation from the rest of your memory. In fact, I often call these memories "freeze-dried" because the experience of the holdup seems to "sit" within your nervous system in its original form. Unlike normal memory, the details do not fade. In fact, you reexperience them each time you have a flashback. Unlike normal memory, these events resist integration into your personal story. In fact, you feel that the holdup has irrevocably altered your story in ways that you cannot control. Therefore, your sense of who you are is shaken. You may have trouble seeing into the future. You are hypervigilant and terribly anxious. You feel sad, depressed, and moody. Your waking consciousness seems to be organized around trying to avoid reexperiencing the memories of the holdup. But you cannot avoid the memories. You cannot forget. You cannot "get over it." This is the classic picture of post-traumatic stress disorder.

As we talk, I would list all of these symptoms and explain that they are the brain's defensive reaction to a life-threatening event. I would explain that you are not losing your mind. You are traumatized and need to heal. And I would tell you that you need an attuned relationship in which to heal. I would explain that you did not become injured alone, and so you cannot expect yourself to heal alone. I would also explain that while this injury seemed to happen in a few seconds, the healing process may take some time. After all, it is not just a "mental" problem.

*The traumatic memory templates have been woven into the very fabric of your mind, emotions, and body. Healing will not be a matter of simply "thinking right."*

This is not really a thinking problem. It is a feeling problem. You are feeling the trauma over and over again in your body as well as your mind, and you need to find ways to heal through the body, the mind, and the emotions—all of which are aspects of the whole experience of living.

I would explain to you that your body is unable to transfer this memory to long-term storage because the emotions that it stirs up every time it is called into consciousness are still too big, too strong, and too intense to be processed normally.

*The goal of our therapy will be to revisit the mugging in a therapeutic way so that the emotions become less intense and the memory of the event can be transferred to normal memory storage.*

"OK," you might say, "how do we do that?"

## Healing from Simple Trauma

Helping someone heal from a simple, one-time trauma is a fairly easy process. I have worked many times with people who were able to recover with just a few sessions of psychotherapy. How was this accomplished? Let us think about this logically. If the trauma became "locked" into the nervous system because the amygdala was overwhelmed by the amount and intensity of the emotion, then any healing method would have to allow this same material to be revisited under conditions of low emotional arousal.

*In other words, you need to go back to the traumatic memory and "go over it" again slowly enough, in a safe enough environment, with enough supportive people around so that you can "take in" the information this time without getting overwhelmed by it.*

In the case of simple trauma, the event is sometimes spontaneously processed over time. Retelling the event in a safe and supportive atmosphere either to a friend, family member, or professional is often an aid in this process. Let us think about an extreme skier who is caught one day in a near-death experience during an avalanche on his favorite mountain. What will he do when he has escaped and returned to the ski village? Is he likely to go home alone without telling anyone about his experience? No, his natural impulse will be to tell the story to his friends and family. Telling the story will help get the information from the amygdala to the hippocampus and into long-term memory stores, where it can be put behind him.

But what if the experience is so shameful it cannot be told? For example, what if a woman is raped at her place of employment? Is she likely to tell anyone? No. It is too embarrassing. So she may feel that she has to keep this experience a secret. Now she cannot use storytelling to recover, at least not with her friends and family. She needs professional help.

*Many different methods for healing from trauma are*
*available within various professional disciplines.*
*All of the methods have in common one key variable:*
*reducing anxiety and arousal while revisiting*
*the original traumatic material.*

I will further discuss healing in chapter 5.

# Summary

Our discussion of stress and trauma, normal and traumatic memory, and simple trauma has drawn distinctions between the way the brain and nervous system process everyday life experiences and the way they process material that is traumatic. We have seen that trauma includes feelings of fear and terror associated with a threat to one's physical or psychological well-being. One's emotional preparedness for a fear-producing event will partially determine whether or not the event can be mastered and produce with it a sense of pride and triumph. Victims, by definition, cannot master the victimizing event. They cannot successfully flee or fight back in a way that gives them a feeling of having mastered the traumatic event. Thus nature, in her mercy, triggers numbing dissociative responses that allow a person to go through a life-threatening event and survive it. The numbed feeling, the alterations in perception of space and time, and the feeling of being "outside" one's own body all contribute to a sense of distance from, and therefore partial safety from, the traumatizing event.

*While nature helps us survive the traumatic event, our current cultural practices often do not allow survivors to heal emotionally from the event.*

The event needs to be revisited under conditions of safety, emotional support from others, and low emotional arousal. In chapter 5 we will discuss some innovative methods to accomplish this healing and some ideas about how the field of psychotraumatology is developing.

# Chapter 5

# Harnessing the Power of Relationship to Heal Emotional Pain

The sales slogan of a popular sportswear company is "Just Do It." Their marketing strategy captures the spirit of the age. "Do it and get it done." "There is no time like the present." "Strike while the iron is hot." "The early bird catches the worm." I could go on and on with sayings and slogans that counsel quick action to yield immediate results.

*Why are there no slogans that urge us to patience*
*or remind us of the slow growth of nature?*

Maybe I should make up some of my own. "You can't make the corn ripe before August," or "Baby peeps don't lay eggs." How about, "No one knows how long the storm will last." They just don't seem to have the same punch, do they? I don't think I could sell too many athletic shoes with those sayings. As you have learned in previous chapters, one-time, isolated simple traumas can often heal easily, even spontaneously, after a relatively short period of time.

However, complex trauma, which is also referred to as a "disorder of extreme stress," is a different story.

*Complex trauma is the result of having been traumatized as a child. Often sufferers not only have experienced childhood abuse like Kim, but they have also suffered repeated traumas throughout their lives.*

Such complex problems do not heal overnight. They are inter-twined with all of the factors we have discussed so far—factors such as attachment style, the ability to form trusting relationships, emotional control, dissociation, and various forms of post-trau-matic stress disorder. When people like Kim come to see me, I some-times have a hard time selling them on the idea that their healing process is going to take a long time. Remember, we are growing the brain, right? If you injure the nerves in your hand by cutting them instead of the carrots you were aiming at, how long do you think it will take for the nerves to be completely healed? It could take years. Compared to skin, which heals very quickly, or to muscles, which also respond pretty quickly, nerve growth is slow. How long does it take a baby to grow a brain? About sixteen years or so, at the very least.

*How long does it take to heal from complex trauma? It depends.*

We'll consider that question as we look more deeply into what is now called disorders of extreme stress.

# Complex Post-Traumatic Stress Disorder

Dr. Bessel A. van der Kolk, a professor of psychiatry at Boston University Medical School and a well-known expert in the field of trauma, has developed an assessment tool that can be used to determine the presence of complex post-traumatic stress disorder. He calls this assessment tool "SIDES," which stands for Structured Interview for Disorders of Extreme Stress. It consists of forty-five questions that deal with six areas of concern which have been shown to be common characteristics of people who have had repeated traumas beginning in childhood. The six areas are (1) problems controlling emotions and impulses, (2) problems with memory, attention, or consciousness, (3) problems in self-perception, (4) problems in relationships with others, (5) inexplicable physical complaints for which doctors can find no cause or cure, and (6) problems with systems of meaning. It became apparent pretty quickly when I began working with Kim that she was having problems in all six areas.

As we have seen from some of Kim's detailed journal entries, she was definitely having difficulty regulating her emotions and impulses. She was in a constant state of emotional distress and was unable to calm or soothe herself. She suffered from unwanted and unwarranted outbursts of strong negative emotions such as fear, terror, anger, and rage. She describes sudden outbursts of terror and fear, wild episodes of reckless driving, and taking risks with her own life. There were also suicidal episodes when she tried to end her life.

Kim was also having trouble with memory, attention, and consciousness. When she first began therapy she could not remember parts of her own story. Her past felt, to her, like a jumbled mass of terrifying emotions and recollections that were so disordered and out of sequence that she had trouble distinguishing fact from fiction. She felt confused about her own life's story. Sometimes she had difficulty keeping track of everyday experiences and often "spaced out" or became numb and detached when she was under stress. Life often felt "unreal" to her, as if she were "just going through the motions."

There were also problems with self-perception. Kim's difficulties with emotion, memory, behavioral control, and consciousness made her feel confused about her own identity. She felt as if she didn't know who she really was. She often felt "invisible," as if she didn't really belong in this life.

*She felt that there was something fundamentally wrong with her, as if she had been "made wrong" from the very beginning. She believed she was "unfixable" and carried a constant feeling of shame and guilt for simply being alive.*

These feelings naturally interfered with Kim's relationships with others. She felt "set apart" from other people, as if she carried a sign on her forehead that said "Defective." She couldn't imagine why anyone would want to have a relationship with her. Her journal entries express surprise that I, her therapist, would want to see her from week to week. She trusted no one and felt terrified of other people, afraid to speak or relate to them. As a result, she spent large portions of her time isolated and brooding, alone in her bedroom, blaming herself for all of her difficulties. When she did try to relate to other people, she often found herself acting in ways that confused or distanced them.

*She simply did not know how to have a good
relationship. However, she did not associate
her childhood experiences with her
present difficulties.*

She kept most of her worst experiences a secret from others. The more she thought about her unacceptability, the more unacceptable she felt. When difficulties arose in her relationships at work, she was unable to be assertive and stand up for her own point of view. She either became enraged and walked out, or she clammed up and quietly allowed others to exploit her.

Physically, Kim felt terrible. She suffered from a variety of physical complaints for which the doctors could find no cause or cure. At different times these symptoms included problems with eating (sometimes overeating and binging and at other times eating almost nothing at all), gastrointestinal difficulties, joint pain, and headaches. During periods of fear and terror, she had panic attacks that included shortness of breath, heart palpitations, and dizziness. At times she had heart pains and imagined she was going to have a heart attack.

*Kim's sense of meaning in life was seriously affected by her
trauma. Her journal entries, as we have
seen, express an overarching sense of self-hatred
and a loss of hope.*

She writes that she feels hopeless and does not believe that her life is meaningful. She does not believe she is an important member of society or that she has a significant role to play. She does not experience a strong sense of satisfaction or pride in her accomplishments.

At different times, she even expresses the feeling that God has abandoned her, although in the later stages of healing, her strong spiritual life and the support of her religious community played a key role in her ability to progress.

So, the causes of Kim's problems were very involved and complicated because she had been traumatized repeatedly in many different ways over a long period of time. It was going to take a long time for Kim to heal.

# The Myth of the Single Cause and the Quick Fix

This chapter takes on the myth of the single cause and the quick fix—the misconception that if you can identify what's wrong you should be able to fix it quickly. The medical model, which dominates much of our thinking, is always looking for a single cause so that a cure can be applied. Got an infection? Take an antibiotic. Got a tumor? You need surgery.

This model works well in medicine when the task is fighting disease. However, Kim didn't have a disease. She wasn't "sick." She wasn't carrying an infection or a cancer. There was no medication or surgical procedure that would instantly "fix" Kim's problem. Her brain had created templates in response to her lifelong emotional experiences.

*Just as she had become wounded over time,*
*she needed to heal over time.*

The healing process was going to parallel the developmental process that had created the templates. It would be fostered by the same factors that foster healthy nervous system development in infants and children. She was going to need the help of a skilled caregiver, attunement with that caregiver in a safe and secure relationship that would be sustained over time, and the opportunity to develop at her own pace. Does this sound familiar? It should, because these are all the things we talked about in chapters 1 through 3. Let's resume Kim's story as she comes to her first psychotherapy appointment.

*On the day of my first appointment, I was so scared. I didn't know what was going to happen. The thought of being in a room alone with one person terrified me. To have someone's attention only on me was too much. I was scared all day and never thought I could do it, but I did make that appointment. It was so hard. I didn't know what I was supposed to do there. When Dr. Pat asked me a bunch of questions about my family and stuff, I couldn't answer. I couldn't even look at her. All I could think of was that I had to get out of there. It was too much to have her looking at me and talking to me. I couldn't even hear what she was saying. All I could hear was my mind thinking how badly I needed to get out of there. I don't think I said anything during that hour. I just kept shaking my head "yes" and "no." The funny thing is, she wanted me to come back in two days. I nodded, "yes."*

Kim came back to see me two days later. I had hoped that her initial silence was simply a matter of nervousness about a new situation. Unfortunately, it was not. Kim remained silent during our second appointment and during all of our subsequent biweekly appointments for the next two years.

Because Kim spent so much time silently listening, I had plenty of opportunities to educate her about the nervous system and trauma. I wanted her to understand how emotional wounding happens, what it does to the mind, body, and emotions, and most importantly, I wanted her to know how to heal. During these first two years that we worked together, she often brought her journal to the sessions. I would silently read it and then talk about how her experiences related to the concepts of the healing process. As she explains in her journal entries,

*What I said was not nearly so important
as the way I said it.*

Kim says that her most vivid recollection from that period is the sound of my voice. During this time we were attuning and forming a bond that would allow her emotional wounds to heal.

As I talked (and talked and talked) in a soothing and understanding voice, I explained the course of the healing journey. I spoke a lot about working with the "forces of the universe" or, in other words, nature and God.

*I explained that healing is a natural process and that our
job was to create a setting and circumstance in which
nature's powerful healing forces could unfold.*

Let's explore some of the concepts I shared with Kim.

# Your Brain Is Repatterning Itself All the Time

One of the first things I explained to Kim was that her brain was always changing. I explained that these changes were dependent upon her experiences. If negative experiences had created her emotional problems, positive emotional experiences could heal them. This was only logical. I reinforced the idea that her brain is not like a machine that just gets built a certain way and that's it. No, the nervous system is more like a plant than like a machine. If you plant a small acorn, eventually it will grow into a mighty oak. At first, it will seem small and delicate. But after it has had time to grow, it will be strong. It will stand the ravages of weather and time.

Kim's first task, then, was to understand that subtle growth processes would characterize the initial phases of the healing process. The internal growth might be so subtle as to be almost imperceptible on the outside.

*The roots of a tree grow underground. Only when the roots are strong enough can the tree manifest itself outwardly with large branches and many leaves.*

I explained to Kim that it was important that she set her expectations for the speed of healing in a way that acknowledged her own developmental processes and the severity of the traumas she had endured. I gave her some guidelines.

# Setting Reasonable Expectations for the Healing Process

I explained to Kim that she needed to base her expectations on her answers to the following questions:

## *Evaluating the Severity of Trauma*

❑ 1. At what age were you hurt? The younger you were, the more serious may be the effects of the trauma.

❑ 2. How long did the trauma go on? The longer the duration, the more serious may be the effects of the trauma.

❑ 3. Did you have a protector you could tell? If not, the effects of the trauma may be more serious.

❑ 4. Were you able to take action to stop the trauma? If not, the effects of the trauma may be more serious.

❑ 5. Did you suffer many traumas and/or many different types of traumas? If so, the effects of the trauma may be more serious.

❑ 6. Was justice ever brought to bear? If not, the effects of the trauma may be more serious.

❑ 7. Was the perpetrator a close friend or relative? If so, the effects of the trauma may be more serious.

❑  8. Did you have a secure attachment experience in child-hood? If not, the effects of the trauma may be more serious.

❑  9. Do you have a support system now? If not, the effects of the trauma may be more serious.

❑  10. Have you been able to integrate the traumatic experi-ences into your own autobiographical story? If not, the effects of the trauma may be more serious.

❑  11. Are you currently in psychological distress? Are these past events affecting your present life—job, family, close relation-ships, enjoyment of everyday life? If so, the effects of the trauma may be more serious.

❑  12. Have you been reenacting the trauma by engaging in self-destructive behaviors? If so, the effects of the trauma may be more serious.

❑  13. Have you recently been retraumatized by another event? If so, the effects of the trauma may be more serious.

❑  14. Do you have another mental illness, a cognitive impair-ment, or a serious health problem? If so, the effects of the trauma may be more serious.

Because you have read some of Kim's story, you know that the effects of her trauma fell at the "more serious" end of the scale on nearly all of the items. Kim had to expect that her healing process would be fairly lengthy and that a significant portion of her early growth and healing would be "underground"—in other words, not readily perceptible in her behavior.

# The Unconscious, Bottom-Up Organization of the Brain

Chapter 1 explains that emotions lie at the center of the brain and, therefore, at the center of our experience of life. This makes it very important to pay attention to what is happening emotionally during the healing process. This may sound simple and obvious, but it is not. Often, methods of psychotherapy emphasize thoughts and thinking over the experience of emotion. Talking itself, which is so often central to psychotherapy, seems to depend upon conscious thought. But, as we see with Kim, during the first two years of her therapy it was not so much what I was saying as the way it was being said that fostered her healing. Even though the healing experience may have been going wonderfully, it was not obvious. Much of Kim's initial healing was subtle and difficult to perceive.

*The process of forming new neural templates is largely unconscious and slowly becomes conscious as the new templates are consolidated and put to use by their "new owner."*

# Attunement

Let's take a look at the entire attunement process and see how Kim and I used its elements in our work together. If you remember what happened with you and baby Matthew, you will recall that an interchange took place between the two of you that sort of "stamped" templates into baby Matthew's brain. Obviously, Kim needed some new templates because the neural templates she had already acquired were based on repeated trauma. She literally did not have the neural templates in place to live a "normal" life. So let's look at attunement. It consists of the following elements:

1. Being aware of bodily sensations and emotions
2. Purposefully directing attention to another person
3. Expressing emotions
4. Keeping emotional arousal levels in the comfortable range
5. Ending the interchange when the baby feels like ending it

Now let's return to Kim and see what she had to say about her internal experience of being in the room with me. Let's see if she was attuning.

*The fear started from the moment I came into her office the first time. Just the thought of sitting in that room with her made my heart beat fast. I started to sweat, and all I could think was that I wouldn't be able to do it. I'm not sure why I even tried to do it. The same thoughts went through my mind over and over again. "What the hell does she want with me anyway? Does she think she can help me? That's a joke. Should I tell her how much I hate myself and everyone and everything else? How most of the time I can't stand to be around people? How everything and everyone scares the hell out of me? How I can't look at or talk to people? How all my life I've wanted to die? What the hell am I going to see her for?" This is what I went through every time I thought of her. It was worse when I was with her. I couldn't look at her or speak to her. I felt terrified and numb. Most of the time she talked and I just nodded "yes" or "no."*

Terrified and numb. Terrified and numb. You have heard that before, too. In chapter 4 we said that the three responses to threat are fight, flight, or, as a last resort, freeze. In one of Kim's journal entries she expresses the urge to flee. She writes, "All I could think of was that I had to get out of there." In this last journal entry she says she felt terrified and numb. So Kim had two out of the three possible reactions to imminent danger—the urge to flee and the feeling of going numb. As her therapist, I guess I should be grateful that she skipped over the desire to fight! Now let's go back to the attunement process and see whether Kim and I could immediately expect to attune. (1) Kim was supposed to be aware of her bodily sensations and emotions, but she writes that she is terrified, feels numb, and wants to run away. (2) She was also supposed to direct her attention to another person (me, her therapist) purposefully. But she writes that she can barely listen to a word I am saying. (3) She is supposed to be expressing emotions, but she says she feels "numb"—she has no emotions to express. (4) Her emotional arousal level is supposed to be kept in the comfortable range. I don't think "terror" qualifies as comfortable. (5) Finally, the interchange is supposed to end when she "feels like" ending it—that is, when bodily sensations and emotions tell Kim she's had enough. Kim felt like ending our interchange before she ever arrived.

So Kim wasn't able to attune with me—not at all, not in any way. She didn't have a prayer of a chance to attune at this point. Let's be clear about this:

> *It isn't that she didn't want to attune*
> *with me—she simply couldn't.*
> *The neural templates weren't there.*

They had not been formed in the first place, or if they were, they had been "pruned" by trauma.

So now what? What were we to do? All too often therapists, friends, and others would try to proceed with Kim from this point as if she were able to attune and would expect her to "just do it." This would be a very bad thing for Kim.

Let's go back to newborns. We said brand new babies really can't attune to anyone else. Other people have to attune to them to show them the way, to help them grow their own "emotional control" templates. So that's where I was with Kim. I needed to attune to her and give her the time to develop.

## My Attunement to Kim

You may be wondering what in the world I talked about twice a week for two solid years during my "silent" sessions with Kim. I talked about the five principles of attunement and about how they applied to Kim. I acknowledged her experience, in the moment, with me. I expressed what I imagined her emotions to be. It wasn't too difficult. She looked terrified.

> *I would say, "You seem terrified." She would shake*
> *her head, "Yes." But I didn't say, "Don't be terrified.*
> *I won't hurt you." That would not be attuning.*

I said, "It is perfectly understandable that you would be terrified of people after all you have been through." Meanwhile, I monitored my own emotions and sensations to try to get "in sync" with Kim. Basically, that meant speaking in the "soft voice" Kim mentions in her journal. I was trying not to scare her. I was attempting with my voice and body language to convey a feeling of safety and comfort to her—in other words, to create a "secure base." Evidently, it worked. Kim wrote in her journal,

> *I started to like going to see Dr. Pat even before I could talk or look at her. She talked to me kindly. No one in a long, long time had talked to me. Because of my inability to talk, we didn't do much "work" for the first two years. Dr. Pat still didn't know too much about me. Since I couldn't talk she gave me a legal pad and asked me to write. I haven't shut up since. I don't know why, but I was able to say a lot when I wrote. I was able to write as if no one would ever see it. I was able to tell her that I've wanted to die all my life. I told her how I hated everything about myself—my looks, my thoughts, my feelings. I was able to tell her how sometimes I want to talk but it makes me so nervous I get too mixed up in my head and I can't think right. I told her that I knew I was born with something bad inside me. I knew God messed up making me. I told her how afraid I am of people. I told her how I knew they could see inside me and see how bad I was inside.*

Kim later wrote,

*During those first years I was able, with a lot of work, to sit there while Dr. Pat read my writing silently, but I could not talk to her about any of it. I looked at the floor, not talking, each session. I don't know what made me keep going back when I couldn't talk or look at her. But she didn't push. Sometimes we sat the whole hour without me saying anything. Since I was seeing her two times a week, I spent the whole week scared, and on the weekend I would start getting nervous about Monday's visit. I don't think that what I felt was always a bad scared feeling. I think part of the fear was because I wanted to trust her. I couldn't figure out why she wanted me to keep coming back. As much as I was sure that neither she nor anyone else could help me, I think I had a little glimmer of hope. At least I was curious as to why she would want to help me. Before every visit, my heart would start beating really hard, I would start to sweat, and I'd start feeling so scared that I would consider turning the car around. I thought I couldn't sit there for another hour. When I got there I was so uncomfortable just walking in. Often I spent most of the visit working on keeping myself from running out the door. I was so uncomfortable just having her (or anyone's) attention on me. I just fidgeted and looked at the floor, nodding my head to answer her questions.*

# The Many Masks of Trauma

A person in the first stage of healing from trauma may wear many masks: a hooker, a drug dealer, a child molester, an alcoholic, a "crazy" person. Often the masks express the trauma metaphorically and "act it out" without the conscious awareness of the sufferer. I can't tell you how many women with anorexia have discovered that they "just can't stomach" what happened to them earlier in life. Or how many people reenact having been beaten as children by beating their own children. Or how many prostitutes have been molested as teenagers. Remember, people make sense. But remember also that neural templates are formed unconsciously. Trauma creates permanent "skyscraper" structures in the brain, not just "weather patterns." The skyscrapers get built and seem to do their thing without the consent of the owner.

*If you or someone you know seems to be doing "crazy things" over and over again, examine their past for "imprints" of relationship patterns in which these "crazy things" began.*

Often the roots are hard to see. They may become obscured by the efforts of the sufferer to cope with them. For example,

*Many victims of trauma eat, drink, or smoke various things to numb themselves to their inner pain.*

Kim told me that she took her first drink when she was eight years old. She said she did it out of curiosity. Her mother had fallen asleep on the couch, drinking this "smelly brown stuff," so Kim tasted it for herself. As time went on, she learned that it gave her a funny feeling that she sort of liked. If she drank enough, it put her to sleep. When her brothers started molesting her, she drank more. She used the alcohol to avoid pain, and it became a habit. Let's return to what she says about it:

> *During my fifteen-year addiction to alcohol and drugs I did a lot of things that could have resulted in a shorter life span. In the neighborhood there was a lake where we used to go swimming. The lake would go over a dam and into a stream about one to two feet deep. The stream had stumps and bottles and trash in it. I used to let the current drag me over the dam to see how far I could safely make it downstream. I would go swimming in January so I could be the first swimmer of the year. I fell through the ice on the lake twice one winter. And at age eighteen I began legally drag racing professionally at some local drag strips. In the five years I did that, I only lost one race. I loved the speed and the fact that if I didn't slow down quickly enough I could run into the woods. My life meant nothing to me.*

In the early stages of her healing process, if you were to ask Kim why she was doing what she was doing, she would have answered, "I have no idea." Her own story and her feelings and actions did not make any sense to her. She couldn't understand her own life or why she was the way she was. Her memory was fragmented, her sense of self disrupted by a personal story that did not make sense.

# Stages of the Healing Journey

We said earlier that a baby's emotional growth occurs in stages, and we said that these stages are arranged hierarchically, meaning that the lower stages of development must occur before the higher stages can be achieved. Each stage builds upon the last. By now it should be no surprise that development during the emotional healing process occurs in the same way. But, just like in the developmental process, the "stages" overlap and sometimes there is a "doubling back" then "moving forward" kind of movement. In other words, progress does not occur in a rigid, linear fashion. Nevertheless, there is an order and an unfolding that takes place. To try to make the process easier to understand, I have divided the healing process into four general stages: Stage 1: Deciding to Get Help and Tuning In, Stage 2: Strengthening and Stabilization, Stage 3: Working Through Traumatic Injuries, Stage 4: Acceptance and Service. Let's take a look at the four stages and consider how the concept of attunement applies during each.

# Stage 1: Deciding to Get Help and Tuning In

*The first task of the first stage of healing is to decide to get help. The second task is to make sure that the help is actually helpful!*

In other words, Kim needed the help of an "attuned caregiver." This is not the same as being tossed about in a fragmented way from one addiction treatment program or short hospital stay to another. These experiences were needed to protect Kim from herself, but they did not really begin the healing journey. They told her that a healing journey was needed. She needed to look for an "attuned caregiver." And she was going to begin to make an association between her "outer" actions, whatever they were, and her "inner" templates. She was going to stop being afraid of herself. In a sense, she decided to stop, turn around, and look herself straight in the eye, finally willing to see whatever it was that she might see. I told her, "Remember, it's not your fault." She was a person with a lot of healing and growing to do, a person in pain, a person confused about who she really was.

Kim needed to look herself in the eye and make the decision to get help. Kim writes of how she arrived at this point:

> I got my first job right after high school, and the drug abuse and drinking skyrocketed. I would get high before work, then at morning break, lunch, then afternoon break. I stayed stoned daily from age seventeen to age twenty-eight. I preferred drugs during the day because they were easier to hide and they didn't make me walk funny or slur my words. I did most of my drinking at home at night. Before I was eighteen my mother moved out of the house and my boyfriend moved in. We were left to care for my three younger siblings.
>
> My boyfriend and I got married after living together for four years. Neither parent was at my wedding. I did not know my father, and my mother informed me that she had to work. I still had not told anyone about my childhood. I did manage to stop drinking while I

*was pregnant. I did stop the drugs for the first trimester but began to smoke marijuana after that. I loved being pregnant. I loved my child so much already, yet I couldn't stay clean. We had a beautiful baby girl in 1983. By the time she turned five years old, I knew she was different. By the time she was six years old, she was classified as multiple handicapped.*

*During this time I was still drinking and doing drugs all day. They were losing their effectiveness. I had to drink more and more and do more drugs to keep those bad feelings down. In mid 1989 I had my first experience smoking cocaine. It was love from the first hit. After that I couldn't get enough of it. There were days that I spent a thousand dollars. I would go to very questionable places to get it, with my daughter in the backseat. I couldn't even wait until I got home to cook it up. I would stop in a grocery store parking lot and get high before I went home. I would leave for work in the morning while it was still dark out so I could park on some back road and get stoned. Cocaine totally controlled me. Prior to the cocaine I never saw my drinking or drug use as a problem. I went to work every day, got great reviews from supervisors, got promotions and raises. There was no problem. Once I started to do cocaine I became a crazy person. When I got high I was paranoid that people were watching me. I began lying to my husband and stealing household money. I knew I had to stop, but when I tried I found I couldn't stop. I would end up at the dealer's seemingly against my will.*

*One day while at work I was stoned and ran into a wall with a forklift, causing five thousand dollars in damage to the wall in addition to the broken truck. I was suspended for three days. This scared me because I knew I couldn't stay home without getting stoned. By this time I knew I had a problem but thought that if I were a good person, a good mother, a good wife, I would be able to stop. I didn't know who to turn to for help because I didn't want anyone else to know what a loser I was. At one point I called my chiropractor, a woman about my age, and told her I had a problem, but quickly recanted. On my second day off, my husband came home from work early with tears in his eyes. He confronted me about my drinking and drug use for the first time. At first I denied it, but soon it was a relief. I ended up in a detox center that evening.*

*I don't remember the three days I spent at the detox center, except for when the social worker told me I had to leave. I cried for the first time in about ten years. I cried uncontrollably. I knew that once I left I would be stoned again. I was scared. The social worker did get me extended two more days, and she looked into inpatient rehabilitation. My insurance would not cover inpatient rehab unless I relapsed first, which I considered. Instead, I chose to go to an outpatient program. Sometime during this twenty-eight-day program I talked about some of the abuse for the first time.*

# Attunement to Self

Kim was much more able to express herself in writing at home, alone because when she was alone in her room she found it easier to keep her emotional arousal system at comfortable levels. She was less likely to go numb and had more access to her own feelings and experiences. As it turns out, Kim is a gifted writer. She had the ability to express herself in writing, and this was a great advantage to her healing journey. Many trauma victims do not have this outlet, and they are just terrified, numb, and speechless. So how can they begin to learn to attune?

*One of the requirements of attunement is awareness of bodily sensation, which is basic to the awareness of emotion.*

Many experts suggest that, for those who are not ready to attune to others due to excessive fear and numbness, exercises and disciplines that help one "tune in" to the body are a great help.

Psychotherapist Babette Rothschild, in her book titled *The Body Remembers,* suggests exercises for paying attention to feeling and sensation. She also offers excellent advice about methods that can help to keep emotional arousal levels within a comfortable range.[7] Psychologist Peter Levine in his book *Waking the Tiger* advises that watching the natural way animals deal with stress and trauma offers a clue for getting in touch with a numb and frozen body. He emphasizes the need to allow the body to shake, rock, tremble, and so forth so that it can "discharge" pent-up emotions and sensations.[8] Kim did, in fact, move around during her sessions with me. Sometimes she would get up from her chair and pace the room as she spoke. At other times she would fold her arms over her chest and rock back and forth in her chair as she spoke. And there were times when her hands would tremble as she recalled her experiences. It was important not to urge her to sit still or to imply that this shaking was somehow a sign that something was wrong. It was actually a sign of nature's trying to help the body and mind heal.

Rothschild, Levine, and others recommend very simple approaches during the initial phases of therapy that are often referred to as "grounding." This includes exercises such as touching one hand with the other and becoming aware of the feeling of that touch, or taking warm baths and showers and focusing attention on the feel of the water as it runs down the back.

*The purpose of these exercises is to begin to control and focus attention on internal experience while keeping arousal levels in the comfortable range and being able to stop the experience when it becomes uncomfortable.*

In other words, these exercises can help develop attunement to self.

I often recommend other approaches that work directly with the body to increase awareness of physical sensation and regulate emotional arousal. Among these approaches are yoga, tai chi, qigong, dance therapy, massage therapy, acupuncture, and other methods that increase bodily awareness in a safe atmosphere and thus promote the healing process.

Medications may also be helpful in keeping emotional arousal levels in a comfortable range for those who suffer from trauma.

*Some antidepressants have been shown to be effective in treating post-traumatic stress disorder, as they tend to keep the emotions on an even keel and help to reduce the depression and anxiety associated with it.*

Edna Foa, Terence Keane, and Dr. Matthew Friedman, editors of the book *Effective Treatments for PTSD,* mention inpatient hospitalization as a form of treatment for post-traumatic stress disorder. During the course of Kim's twelve-year treatment she had about five short-stay inpatient hospitalizations. Most of them occurred during the initial phases of treatment, and they became less frequent as treatment progressed. Hospitalization was necessary whenever her desire to end her own life became uncontrollable. She needed to be in the hospital for her own safety. It was also a good time to try medications that helped to control her symptoms. Unfortunately, Kim's inpatient experiences were not always pleasant. When the inpatient staff understood trauma and its effects, the hospital stay not only kept her physically safe, it often promoted the healing process. When the hospital staff did not understand—or, worse, did not "believe in" trauma and its effects—her experience in the hospital was both unpleasant and unproductive. One of the worst effects of a hospital stay with those untrained in trauma is that it made Kim reluctant to go back to a hospital the next time her symptoms became unbearable. It was important to try to find a suitable hospital when inpatient treatment was necessary. Happily, trauma theory is becoming more and more mainstream. In large metropolitan centers it is often possible to find an inpatient unit that specializes in treatment of trauma victims.

## Stage 2: Strengthening and Stabilization

In the second stage of healing from trauma, the strengthening and stabilization phase, Kim stopped all of the unhealthy things she was doing either to avoid or to act out the traumatic experiences. It was particularly important to stop all of her addictive behaviors. It was also important to realize that stopping an addiction was not an end in itself but only a step along the way to healing.

In this second stage of healing, the goal of attunement is to become aware of bodily sensations and emotions and to learn how to keep emotional arousal levels in the comfortable range. Rothschild calls the process of focusing on bodily sensation to reduce emotional arousal "putting on the brakes." This stage is difficult. People in this stage are learning a new way of being that is totally foreign to their previous experience. Remember how awkward it felt to learn something new, like driving a car or swinging a golf club? Imagine how awkward it would feel to try to recalibrate your whole way of reacting to other people and to yourself. Obviously, it doesn't happen overnight. Patience and steadfastness are the keys to this stage of development. Remember that Kim and I sat together through over two hundred sessions before she even said anything, and this was after she had stopped her addictions. I explained to Kim that she could expect during this stage that emotional expression would be misattuned for the most part.

*Fear from the past would rear its ugly head and cause her body to react with fight-or-flight and freeze responses. These responses might be very unpredictable and confusing.*

Kim's current life circumstances had to become safe and stable before she could proceed to the next stage, in which the issues of the past would be addressed. It would have been very unwise to enter stage 3, which can be stressful, while everyday life was still in crisis and chaos. Continuing to take medications that were helping her was also important to treat coexisting psychiatric problems and to help stabilize her emotions.

Perhaps the most important task of all in stage 2 was for Kim to arrange her daily life so that she was in a safe, supportive environment. A battered woman, for example, cannot recover from past trauma if she is still being battered. An emotionally abused child cannot heal from this relationship harm if he or she is still living within the context of that harm on a daily basis. At the time she entered treatment, Kim was living by herself in a roach-infested apartment above a married couple who fought daily. Every day the husband would beat his wife, and Kim was witness to the sounds of domestic violence. Furthermore, the neighborhood was riddled with drug activity. For obvious reasons this environment was not a good place for Kim to begin her healing. When she moved to a better, safer place, she was able to begin moving forward with her healing work.

Stages 1 and 2 are not easy and may take a long time, depending on the severity of the trauma and on the availability of supportive relationships and a "secure base." Kim needed reassurance that taking a long time did not mean she was not making progress.

*I urged her not to confuse slowness of progress with failure, to keep going, and to remember that her brain was growing.*

Here is what Kim had to say about the second stage of her healing journey:

*During the second year of therapy I was able to talk a very little about what Dr. Pat had read silently. At least I was able to give short answers to questions she asked. I still couldn't look at her, and I still spent the whole visit feeling uncomfortable and trying not to run out. By the third year I would be able to sit there while Dr. Pat read aloud what I wrote, and then I'd try to discuss it to the best of my ability. That was very, very hard. Sometimes I would become too overwhelmed and she'd have to stop reading. I don't know why that was so hard. Hearing my inner thoughts made me extremely nervous. Maybe hearing them read aloud just reinforced that I was sharing it with Dr. Pat. Maybe that's what made me so nervous. I believed my thoughts and feelings were wrong, or sick, and here I was sharing them. Maybe the fear was that I believed that after I shared myself with her she would hurt me or leave me. I spent years waiting for that to happen, and I realize now that sometimes I did things to make her leave. Not intentionally, but I broke our agreements. I guess I thought it would be easier to give her a reason to leave than to have her leave me for nothing.*

# Stage 3: Working Through Traumatic Injuries

In Kim's last journal entry, it is apparent that she has been in therapy for over three years. It's also clear that the traumas of the past have not yet been directly addressed. She was not ready for that. However, this does not mean that progress had not been made. Quite the contrary—tremendous growth in her emotional control system had occurred because she now felt that she was ready to deal with the past. But there are some guidelines for dealing with old traumas.

First and foremost, it is important to keep in mind the hierarchical nature of development. A child who tries to walk before crawling will fall down and get hurt. So, too, with trauma work.

*Much damage and discouragement can result from insisting that a traumatized individual "just talk and get it out" before they are ready.*

This is the "just do it" approach. Unless the time is right, attempting this may make matters worse instead of better. For example, if we were to go back to Kim when she was hospitalized for the first time for her addictions and return to the moment when she first connected her addictions to the abuse she had suffered, we can imagine that some people at the hospital may have thought she should be "encouraged," confronted, and made to talk about the abuse. This would have caused further harm. Why? You already know why, right? Her nervous system was not equipped to handle it yet.

The second thing to remember is that simply talking about the trauma will not heal it. By "talking about it" I mean reporting it like a newscaster without an emotional connection to the story. Remember, it is not so much what happened in the past (the facts, the "video replay" of the trauma) but the effect of this event that is troublesome.

We were going to revisit events that remained unresolved for Kim—events that were causing problems right that very minute. The task, then, during this phase of therapy in which the past would be revisited was not to find out the facts per se. Strange as it may seem, the facts were not the issue. I am not saying that they were not important. I am saying they were not the issue at hand. It was the impact of the events, or Kim's emotional experience of the events, that counted.

So what were we going to do about these old traumatic experiences? Perhaps you have already guessed that we were going to attune to them. That's right. Think about it again with me. Attunement consists of the following elements:

1. Being aware of bodily sensations and emotions
2. Purposefully directing attention to self or other
3. Expressing emotions
4. Keeping emotional arousal levels in the comfortable range
5. Stopping the interchange when the emotional intensity becomes too great

So that is what we did to deal with Kim's trauma. When Kim and I felt the time was right, we planned a time to meet to begin this work. We set up this plan ahead of time and gave Kim an opportunity to prepare for it mentally and emotionally. We had a specific goal for the meeting. We identified a specific trauma or event that we were going to address, and Kim knew ahead of time what procedure we were going to use to address it. All of this preparation was, I believe, every bit as important as what happened during the planned session itself.

*Remember, suddenly shocking, surprising, or overwhelming Kim with emotional experiences that she was not prepared to handle would not have helped her heal.*

In fact, such experiences would very likely have had the opposite effect and would have compounded her trauma. So very careful attention to planning was necessary as Kim headed into the part of therapy that would include dealing with past traumas.

Another key concept during this phase was pacing. By pacing I mean, again, not overwhelming Kim. Normally, I do a trauma memory session and follow it with one or more sessions during which we talk about what happened during the trauma memory session.

If this process sounds pretty tricky, it is. Remember that the trauma is associated with overwhelming emotion—that's what makes it traumatic in the first place. If we were simply to bring up the trauma and expose Kim to that same overwhelming emotion again, it would have harmed her instead of helping her. This is basically what happens during a flashback. The harm of the past is reexperienced.

So what to do? Well, different approaches can be taken. At the end of the book I have listed texts that discuss the latest methods that have research to back them up.

*One of the most promising methods that is backed by research is called Eye Movement Desensitization Reprocessing, or EMDR. It is effective because it creates the structure and process of attunement to the trauma.*

I will give you a brief overview of this method; however, this is not the only method available. It is one of many tools that can be used to treat trauma.

# Eye Movement Desensitization and Reprocessing

Eye Movement Desensitization and Reprocessing, or EMDR as it is commonly called, is a technique that was developed specifically for use in recovery from traumatic experiences. The technique integrates elements of several successful psychotherapies in a structured process that is designed to maximize the effects of the treatment. Its originator, Dr. Francine Shapiro, discovered the technique and quickly began applying it clinically in her work with veterans of the Vietnam War. The technique soon proved successful and sparked a body of research in support of its effectiveness. The technique is very compatible with the concepts we have discussed so far. It requires careful planning of a session in which traumatic emotional material will be addressed. It requires that the therapist and client set up a "protocol" that will ask the client to be aware of bodily sensations, emotions, thoughts about themselves, and a numerical rating of the level of emotional arousal stimulated by thinking about the trauma. This numerical rating will be used during the session to rate the progress of trauma resolution.

For example, I did an EMDR session with Kim that addressed her brother's daily teasing and harassment of her. I began the session by asking Kim to rate on a scale of one to ten her level of emotional distress as she recalled those traumatic events from the past. I asked, "How do you feel now when you think of those events then?" Kim said that she felt a level of emotional distress of ten on a scale of one to ten, with zero being no emotional distress at all and ten representing a nearly unbearable amount of distress. As Kim and I began our session, she could not imagine that her goal of being able to think about this event from the past with an emotional distress level of zero could actually be accomplished in a ninety-minute therapy session. In fact, that is exactly what occurred. We accomplished the goal by breaking her memory of the trauma down into small, "bite-size" morsels of emotional experience, processing them by being aware of her thoughts, her bodily sensations and her emotions, and moving on to the next "morsel." The technique includes some form of repetitive sensory stimulation such as eye movements or repetitive tones in between each "morsel" of traumatic experience.

In Kim's case, I placed earphones in her ears and played a tone that alternated rhythmically between the right ear and the left ear. I have also used a light that flashes from the right to the left instead of the alternating tone. By breaking the traumatic memory up into these smaller segments, which are interspersed with the sensory stimulation, emotional arousal is kept at comfortable levels that allow a previously overwhelming experience to be revisited and processed so that it can be transferred to "normal" memory as we discussed in chapter 4.

Let's see what Kim had to say about her EMDR experiences:

> *Eventually I was able to gradually tell Dr. Pat about my childhood through the use of EMDR and relaxation exercises. I had never forgotten it. I just couldn't say the words. I had mentioned it in the drug rehabilitation program many years ago. I knew my childhood was the reason I always felt horrible about myself. I was a little scared about doing this work. I was afraid that I would lose all control, but I didn't. I was mainly just very relaxed. I began to actually look forward to the sessions. I finally had a voice. I began to see where all*

*my pain was coming from. It was finally, slowly, getting released. And I was getting comfort while it was getting released. That's what I never had, a chance to release and let go of all my old pain.*

*Before the EMDR, I would tear up my arms with a knife. It eased the pain inside when I felt pain outside. Sometimes I did it just to feel anything. Sometimes I was so without feeling that I felt as though I weren't really here. I wrote this poem around that time:*

> *I never laughed,*
> *I never cried.*
> *I never lived,*
> *I never died.*
> *I existed.*
> *I survived.*

## Other Methods for Processing Trauma

There are, of course, other methods of treating survivors of trauma. The International Society for Traumatic Stress Studies has published a review of the field of trauma treatment titled *Effective Treatments for PTSD*. The book surveys various techniques and approaches and offers a review of the literature on their current status as scientifically sound treatments. The volume states, "currently, there are no clear guidelines for choosing among treatment modalities."[9] However, it offers several guidelines for making choices and reminds the reader that expected effectiveness should be the first criterion for choosing a mode of treatment for post-traumatic stress disorder.

*Evidence for the efficacy of EMDR in treating
post-traumatic stress disorder is growing.*

Other treatment modalities that are used in hospitals and other treatment programs include use of medications, cognitive-behavioral therapy, group therapy, hypnosis, marital and family treatment, psychodynamic therapy, psychosocial rehabilitation, and creative therapies including movement therapies such as art, music, dance/movement, drama, and poetry in psychotherapy. These methods are reviewed in the book. In addition to EMDR, Kim's healing journey included medication, journaling, and psychotherapy to address her trauma. She took medication for her mood problems and has continued in a twelve-step program to address addictions. Her spiritual life also contributed greatly to the healing process as I will describe in the next chapter. Further information on how survivors of trauma can find the help they need can be found in the appendix. Each individual must choose the constellation of treatment approaches that seems best for his or her situation.

## Triggers and Reenactments

Throughout all phases of the healing journey the phenomena of triggers and reenactments of the traumatic experience can plague the survivor of post-traumatic stress disorder. Neural templates that recorded the traumatic experience replay at unwanted times in inappropriate situations. This is one of the more irksome and distressing symptoms of post-traumatic stress disorder. Let's see what Kim has to say on this topic.

*I was even extremely afraid when I was alone, with no one near me to be afraid of. I would pace around my house feeling like a caged animal. Feeling like my head was just going around and around. I couldn't make sense of my thoughts or my feelings. I wanted to hit something some of those times. My heart would be beating fast and I would be breathing hard. I felt like my head would explode, there was so much going on in there. I couldn't think straight.*

Kim describes a situation in which she is all alone and yet has a physical reaction similar to that of a person about to be eaten by a tiger. She is "extremely afraid," she feels like "fighting," and she says she wants to "hit something." Her rapid heartbeat and breathing suggest that she is deeply into a fight-or-flight or freeze reaction, but notice that she says she is simply walking around her own house, completely alone. What in the world is this all about? This is about what the literature on trauma calls "triggering."

*To be "triggered" is to experience the bodily sensations and emotions of a terrifying event that happened long ago. To be triggered is to reexperience an event from the past in the present.*

It is a frightening experience, and unless one knows the cause, it can make a person feel as if they are going crazy. The emotions may be out of control and unrelated to present experience.

When I am in court trying to explain to judges and jurors what a trigger is, I often use the example of the Vietnam War veteran with post-traumatic stress disorder. Some veterans from the Vietnam War were so traumatized that any loud noise similar to the sound of a gun will trigger flashbacks of the war. Grown men have been known to roll into a gutter next to the street to "take cover" from the sound of a car backfiring. The sound triggers a full-body reenactment of the war experience.

This reenactment is not under the veteran's conscious control. This response just happens automatically when the neural network associated with the trauma of the war is triggered. This idea no longer seems strange when we think about other automatic neural networks we have discussed. From smiling to get attention to swinging a golf club, we know that once something is imprinted in the neural circuits, it becomes a part of you. I told Kim that the best thing to do about triggers was to try to identify the kinds of things that triggered her and avoid them when she could. Second, I encouraged her to develop a plan to deal with triggers. Aphrodite Matsakis, in her book *I Can't Get Over It: A Book for Trauma Survivors*, recommends that the survivor prepare a written dialogue to read to herself when this happens. She suggests that the dialogue include reminders that (1) this is just "old stuff"—a triggering experience, (2) that she can ride it out—it will pass, (3) that she is safe, and (4) to pay attention to breathing and to doing things that bring feelings of comfort. [10]

# Rage

One of the most bothersome types of triggers is that which brings the feeling of rage along with it. Kim wrote in her journal that when these triggering experiences would occur, she felt as if she "wanted to hit something." She was full of rage. She told me that she carried so much hatred and anger inside that she was afraid if she ever started to let it out, it might get out of control. She was afraid she would hurt me if she just tried to talk about how she really felt inside. Here, pacing and going slowly are key, but not backing away is also key. If you are blocking rage, you are also blocking all other emotions along with it.

*Rage, like all strong emotions, can be dealt with in the ways we have discussed.*

Attuning to rage, though, can sometimes be pretty disruptive. I will tell a quick story about that.

One time when I was in Nova Scotia giving a lecture to a group of survivors of childhood abuse, I wrote the word "RAGE" on the blackboard as I began to explain the things I have just explained to you. As the word settled onto the chalkboard, one of the women in the audience jumped up and screamed at me, "Get that RAGE off that board! I can't stand to sit here and see my rage out there for everyone to see!" Then she angrily stomped out of the room. I was stunned, as was the rest of the audience. Luckily, we were in a small group setting and were able to stop the lecture, invite the woman back into the room, and support her while she talked about her rage. Later in the weekend, she thanked me and the other participants for helping her break through to her blocked and raw emotions. Even now, I remember her and her courage that weekend.

# Taking a
# Developmental
# Perspective

As Kim began to think about doing the trauma work, I suggested that she might wish to make a timeline of her life. She listed each of the major traumas that had occurred at various stages of her life. As we began the healing work, we addressed the developmentally early traumas first. This can sometimes help to speed the healing process, as healing early trauma can sometimes "automatically" heal the later traumas that are basically reenactments of the original traumatic templates.

Although there are four stages of healing, they are organically related to one another, meaning that progress forward will include "doubling back" to earlier tasks. Old learning and new learning integrate and change behavior in the here and now. This is an exciting process. It is a time of change, challenge, and rapid growth. I caution the people I work with to respect the nature of this rapid healing time. It is like the first few months after open-heart surgery. You wouldn't be expected to do too much during those months except heal from the operation. Well, working through old traumas is like a heart operation. It is a time to reduce stress and to respect the difficulty of the process. As Kim moved through the process of facing and dealing with the past, she emerged into stage 4, acceptance and service.

# Stage 4: Acceptance and Service

If the hallmark of stage 1 is the noise, chaos, and inner confusion of dissociated thought, feeling, and emotion, the hallmark of stage 4 is peace of mind. Acceptance is the key word. By the time Kim moved into stage 4, she was no longer hiding from her true self, her past, her real feelings. Now she could embrace her story as part of what makes her who she is. She was no longer letting her emotions hold her hostage. She had developed emotional control and the ability to think before she acted. When triggers arose, she was able to recognize them. She had a well-practiced strategy for coping with them and recovering quickly. Her inner life was no longer dominated by feelings of rage toward herself and others. She had begun to form the capacity for warm, loving relationships because she had developed a warm and loving attitude toward herself. She had begun to see herself within her own story with compassion and empathy. She was becoming the heroine of her own story.

From this new perspective of compassion, Kim no longer felt like an "oddball" who had suffered wrongs that kept her alienated from others, but rather she saw her own suffering as a part of the pain and anguish that all mankind must bear. Her pain had opened her heart so that she could feel, see, and understand so much about the private pain of others. She had developed a strong desire to help others as she had been helped.

As Kim moved more fully into stage 4, the aspects of her internal life that had changed began to manifest themselves in the world. Relationships changed. Harmful ones were discarded or avoided while new, positive connections grew in their place. New goals and directions in life emerged. At this stage, all of those self-help books that had once seemed useless became potentially helpful. Even the advice to "just get over it" no longer smarted.

> *"I have gotten over it," Kim told me.*
> *"I'm moving on."*

If all of this seems just too good to be true, I assure you it is not. This is the reward at the end of the journey. Kim has said it best. "You know," she said, "I just realized the other day, I can do anything I set my mind to. I can be anything I want." Wow. "And you know what else?" she said. "I am glad to be alive. I really want to live. I never thought I would say that!"

Even now, Kim continues her healing journey. She remains very active in a twelve-step program, attending three to five meetings per week and sponsoring other women in recovery. She frequently serves as a speaker for meetings, and her healing story has been an inspiration to many.

## Summary

This chapter has addressed the myth of the single cause and the quick fix. It has shown that childhood abuse, neglect, abandonment, and stress leave lasting scars and a constellation of symptoms that can affect all aspects of life.

Our discussion has shown that healing from prolonged and complicated traumatic experiences occurs in a four-stage process that requires attunement between the caregiver and the survivor of trauma. Stage 1 involves deciding to get help, finding an attuned caregiver, and attunement to oneself. Stage 2 is a period of strengthening and stabilization. Stage 3 is the "working through" stage when trauma finally gets processed, and stage 4 is one of acceptance, service, and peace of mind. The attunement process provides a simple model and guideline for the ideal therapeutic relationship. It also offers a model that can be used to address specific traumas by revisiting them under conditions of low emotional arousal and safety. Though there are many other therapeutic approaches, the method I have found to be most effective is EMDR.

Disturbances in meaning and in one's religious life and personal philosophy are often part of the problem with post-traumatic stress disorder. This is the subject of chapter 6, "Belief, Blame, and God," which takes on the myth that God is like a vending machine doling out good stuff to the good and bad stuff to the bad. Chapter 6 explores the widespread cultural belief that victims are to blame for their own suffering.

# Chapter 6

# Belief, Blame, and God

THE PREVIOUS CHAPTERS HAVE DRIVEN HOME the point that relationships and other life experiences change the structure of your brain and the way it functions. We have discussed the positive, growth-producing experiences of attunement in infancy and have shown how these experiences form a bedrock, a "secure base," upon which a child's self-image, sense of self-confidence, and emotional maturity grow. We have seen through the story of Kim that lack of attunement and lack of a secure base in her early years made her vulnerable to traumatic injury. Kim, without a protector to whom she could turn when she was being hurt, was left to fend for herself. Many people took advantage of her. As her trauma increased, her sense of self-control and self-worth decreased. Eventually, she was emotionally bankrupt and wished her life to end.

We have discussed the processes of Kim's healing in terms of the new relationship experiences she needed in order to "grow her brain" in ways that would allow her to feel differently about herself. We have speculated about the importance of the psychotherapeutic relationship and its ability to give Kim the attunement and safety that would allow her to heal. Now we are going to turn our attention to three other extremely important aspects of Kim's healing journey. This chapter will address the issues of belief, blame, and God.

# It's Just All in Your Head

Many years ago, I was working with a woman, whom I will call Marla, in rural Kentucky. Marla had a history similar to Kim's. Marla's mother was a single, unmarried teenager when Marla was born, and Marla had never met her father. While Marla was growing up, her mother worked full time for a professional cleaning service in the evening, so she was seldom home when Marla came home after school. When Marla was ten, her mother got married, bringing a stepfather into Marla's life. The stepfather emotionally and sexually abused Marla. Although Marla told her mother about the abuse, her mother did nothing to stop it because she did not believe Marla. She said Marla was just being "manipulative" and making up stories because she didn't like her stepfather.

Over the years, Marla, like Kim, sometimes became so despondent and exhausted from trying to cope with the abuse and all of the emotional pain that it caused that she would become hopeless and would try to end her own life. During about a fifteen-year period Marla had attempted suicide four times. Each time, she was rescued, picked up by the local ambulance squad, taken to the local emergency room, and then admitted to the psychiatric ward for a few days. In a short time, usually less than three or four days, she would profess to be "fine." She would be released, urged to get help, and sent home. Then her life would continue much the same as before. Because she lived in a very small rural community, everyone in town knew Marla and something of her unstable family life and her emotional ups and downs. In this small town, Marla had come to be known by the local police and rescue workers as "a head case."

About a week after the September 11, 2001, World Trade Center bombing, Marla again became despondent and took an overdose of Tylenol. She called her best friend to say "Good-bye." Her friend suspected the worst and called the local rescue squad. The rescuers broke into Marla's home, found her sleeping, and took her to the emergency room. Later that same day, I received a call from Marla, who told me the story of her day. I was astonished to learn that she was calling me from home! I asked her why the emergency room had released her. She said she didn't know, but she was glad she didn't have to be admitted to the hospital as she had on other occasions. I hung up the phone, called the emergency room, and asked to speak to the doctor who had evaluated her and sent her home. The doctor said that the blood tests showed she had not taken a toxic dose of Tylenol and that there was no reason to keep her. He said, and I quote, "I told her that there was nothing wrong with her. Her problems were all in her head."

I wish I could tell you that this kind of negative attitude toward people with psychological problems is unusual and limited in scope. I don't believe it is. I have lived in big cities and in small communities. I have worked with folks from all around the country, and I hear the same kind of stories over and over again.

*In the medical community, among insurance providers, and in society at large "psychological" problems are seen as less real and less legitimate than problems seen as "physical."*

It is a curious thing. We don't blame diabetics for being diabetic, nor do we blame cancer patients for having cancer. But isn't it true that we often blame people like Kim and Marla for being so "messed up"? Don't we often think that, really, if they just tried a little harder they could pull themselves up by the bootstraps and "get it together"?

I think so, and there is some interesting research to back up my observation. It comes from an area in social psychology called "attribution theory."

*Attribution is the study of the sense people make of things that happen in their lives—that is, what they think events mean and what they think caused the events to happen.*

For Kim and so many like her, their attribution of the meaning of their suffering is that they themselves are to blame. Let's take a look at what Kim had to say about this during a session that occurred about four years into her therapy.

## God Is Not a Vending Machine

Kim came into my office for her scheduled appointment, and we had a conversation that went like this:

"I have decided to give up," Kim said.

"Give up what?" I asked.

"Living," she answered.

"Give up living? What are you talking about?" I asked.

"I have decided I don't really belong here at all," she answered.

"Here? Where? In Mesopita County?"

"No, on earth," she answered.

She was looking down now, staring at the floor. She had tears in her eyes.

"Kim, what's up? I don't understand what you are saying," I said softly.

"I am saying that I've decided that my being here on earth was some sort of mistake. I don't know how these mistakes happen, but in my case it seems pretty clear that I don't belong here. Look at all the things that have happened to me. My mother didn't want me, I was neglected, and finally abandoned. I was abused by nearly everyone who was ever close to me. The bad things just keep happening. The pain won't go away. My suffering is proof that I am bad, made wrong. If I were made right, things would be going right. They are not. I am not. I quit. That's all. I am just tired of trying to make something broken work. I am broken, and I am bad."

"Kim," I said, "you are saying that you know you are bad because bad things have happened to you. You are talking as if God were like a huge vending machine in the sky. What do you think— that if you do the right things, good stuff comes out?"

Kim answered, "Well, kind of, yes."

"So you are saying you get what you deserve. You are to blame if you happen to have been born into a home where you were not loved. It is your fault that as an infant, you were neglected. It is your fault that your brothers abused you. And the proof is that you suffered then and you still suffer, which is also your fault. You suffer because you were made wrong, and the proof is that you suffer. This is all a big circle, Kim. I am bad because I suffer, and I suffer because I am bad."

"No," she said. It isn't just that I am hurting. It is because I prayed to God to stop all the hurt, and He didn't. So now I know that even God thinks I am bad. He didn't answer my prayers."

"Well, Kim, maybe God did hear your prayers. You are here," I said.

"There you go again," she said. "I *know* I am *here*. What does that have to do with it? I wish you would be serious."

"I am serious," I said, trying harder to attune my emotions, "very serious. What are you doing here, right now, with me?"

"Trying to get better," she said.

"Right," I said. "And are you getting better?"

"I guess," she said begrudgingly, as if she thought I were trying to trick her into something.

"Did you ever think back then that it would be possible? Did you ever think back then that you would know someone like me, someone who is trying to help you? Did you wish for it from God, but not really believe it could be so?"

"Well, yeah," she said. "I see what you mean. I really knew I was trash then. I knew no one would ever care about me."

"So, you prayed to God to stop the abuse, and it has stopped. And you prayed to God to heal, and you are healing." I stated it simply and looked at her.

"The problem is that I am thirty-eight years old and I am not better *yet*," she said angrily. "I am sick of it."

"Oh, so the problem is time—it is taking too *long* for God to answer your prayers. You do want a vending machine. In with the prayer—out with the prize. Zam, bam. Done."

"Yeah," she said, although I could see she was beginning to soften a little.

"Kim," I took her hands and looked her right in the eye, "who do you think needs all this time for healing?"

She looked back at me, eye-to-eye. "I don't know," she said. "Me, I guess."

I continued to look Kim in the eye. "For three years now I have been telling you that God has not abandoned you, not now, not ever. For three years I have been telling you that you are not bad, not now, not ever. And tell me, have you believed me?"

"No," she answered.

"No," I said. "Not yet. Not yet, but you will. Every once in a while, especially lately, you consider at least the possibility that it might be so. The strength of that possibility is growing. But, just about the time you seem to be ready to embrace it, you lash back at yourself with every bit of force you have to the contrary. Like to-day. You pay yourself back for every step forward with a big slap back. You have come in here many weeks and asked me, 'Aren't you getting sick of me yet?' Are you hopeful that I am? Are you hopeful that finally you will be able to return to your familiar conviction that you are bad and that people, and God, are sick of you? Every week I disappoint you and say, 'No, I am never sick of you. Why would I be?' The one who is sick of taking so much time is you, you see. Healing goes as fast or as slow as our minds and hearts can handle it. Speed is not a concern of God, nor is my concern, for that matter. Time is something we think is real because we humans on the planet here wear watches and look at calendars. But what is time anyway? Think about it. Remember your best friend from first grade that you told me about? Remember when you bumped into her in the supermarket the other day and recognized her after thirty-two years? Remember what you said about that meeting?"

"I said it was like we were together just the other day. We knew each other. We were still best friends."

"Right. That's what you said. So what about time? What did the time do?"

"Nothing."

"Right, because you love each other. Love is a force, a timeless, shapeless, invisible force that is stronger and more real than anything."

She was still looking me in the eye.

"You are here today. You are healing. You see in my eyes, what?"

"That you care," she answered. "I still have trouble believing that, but that is what I see when I can look."

"You have trouble believing."

"Yes."

"So what is the problem? Is it the idea that God doesn't care for you, or is it your not being able to believe that anyone, including God, cares? Is it God, or is it your belief?"

I was still looking her in the eye.

"Hum," she said.

Kim nodded her head, realizing the irrationality of her thoughts, but not budging from them either. Something inside her was telling her that this was all her fault—all her fault that she was abandoned by her father, neglected by her mother, physically and sexually abused by her brothers, and so on.

I argued with her on that day and on many other days over the course of the years of her healing. Again and again I have had to explain to Kim that the things she had suffered were *not her fault*. At first, she didn't believe me, but over time, as she began to feel better about herself, the realization that I am right eventually seeped in. In fact, I recently asked Kim about our work over our many years together. I asked her if she were to sum up our work in a few sentences what she would say. What is it that we really did together? She answered quickly and easily, "You helped me realize it wasn't my fault. Before I believed that, I couldn't get better. I blamed myself and believed I deserved everything that had happened to me and deserved to suffer for it for the rest of my life. I hated myself, you see. I really, really hated myself for all that had happened in the past."

# The Fundamental Delusion: Belief in a Just World

The question of blame is important in the process of healing from trauma. Notice that Kim said she "blamed" herself. The key to her healing was to realize that she did *not* deserve what had happened to her and that it wasn't her fault that she had been neglected and abused.

For many years Melvin Lerner, a pioneering social psychologist, has studied the question of who is responsible for the suffering of the innocent. He has been particularly interested in this question of "attribution," or the meaning people make of the changing circumstances of their lives. His research has looked at questions such as what is the cause of getting a raise at work. When you get a raise, do you attribute this event to your own hard work or to good luck? If you fall on the ice, do you attribute your accident to your clumsiness or to the failure of the snow removal crew? And if you are a victim of abuse, who do you blame?

According to Lerner's research,

*People tend to put the blame for suffering on the people who are victims of that suffering rather than blaming the sufferer's circumstances.*

Lerner's research, which has been replicated many, many times over the past thirty years, shows that even when people have evidence to the contrary, they tend to blame victims for being victims. It seems that people want to believe that the world is a just place and that people generally get what they deserve and deserve what they get.

This theory is known as the "Just World Hypothesis," which Lerner labels a "fundamental delusion."[11] Let me share with you some of Lerner's findings.

In one of his studies, college students were asked to watch through a one-way mirror while a fellow student was being shocked with electricity. The observing students were told to watch closely and to pay attention to the emotions of the student who was being shocked. The observers saw the research subject receive a series of electric shocks that caused visible distress and suffering. While the observers reported that at first they were upset by the victim's suffering, as the experiment progressed and the observers could do nothing to stop the suffering, they began to blame the victim. The results showed that the more the victims were seen to suffer, the more they were blamed for their suffering. In other words, the greater the injustice, the greater the tendency to denigrate the victim.

Lerner's early explanations of his research findings centered around the idea that people need to believe the world is a just place so that they can feel safe and in control of their own lives. He said that

*We need to believe that bad things happen to* other *people because of the wrong things they are doing and that these bad things will not happen to us because we are doing the right things.*

However, despite the attractiveness of this belief, it is an error. Bad things happen to perfectly innocent people all the time.

Throughout history we can see this attribution error in action. We see that African Americans were often blamed for their own enslavement. Women were blamed for their own oppression. Victims of crime have sometimes been blamed for not being more careful or for being in the wrong place at the wrong time. Lerner and others found that this tendency to blame the victim stood up in a wide range of circumstances and research designs over a long period of time. However, as his research progressed, he found that under certain research conditions, the tendency to blame the victim could be reversed. In studies in which he told the observers of suffering to put themselves in the other person's shoes, the tendency to blame the victim disappeared. In these studies, innocent victims of suffering were seen as innocent. Blame was correctly assigned to the circumstances. In other words, attuning to the victim and having empathy for the victim reversed the attribution error!

These results led Lerner to the belief that we all carry within us two ways of looking at things. On the one hand, at a very deep, unconscious, emotional level, we never really lose our childhood, fairy-tale belief that the good guys always win and that the bad people suffer. But, on the other hand, most adults in their conscious mind know differently. They know that "bad things happen to good people," as the title of the book by Harold S. Kushner suggests.[12] But, Lerner says, they have to *think* in order to remember this. We have to make the effort to attune to others and put ourselves in their shoes. We have to have empathy.

Kim's case illustrates one of the reasons why this question of attribution is such a key point. When Kim was traumatized by her family and others, she was told that it was her fault. They told her she was bad and deserved this kind of treatment. They told her this in the same breath that they told her not to reveal these events to anyone because no one would believe her and if they did, they would put the blame on her. We can readily see that this was a strategy Kim's abusers employed to keep her quiet about what they were doing, but it took Kim a very long time to see and understand this.

The questions raised by the suffering of the innocent seem best answered from a spiritual perspective. Why does evil exist in the world? Why do the innocent suffer? Psychology leaves these most vexing of life's questions to the philosophers and religious teachers.

## The Spiritual Sanctuary

In order to weather the storms of blame and trial and tribulation that the world so frequently offers those on the healing journey, many turn to the world of religion for refuge. Here, if all goes well, they find a loving community of people who can understand their trials and provide support and understanding. Within faith communities there is a widespread understanding that suffering and innocence often go hand in hand. The founders of all the world's major religions endured suffering while they were on earth. From political reformers like Mohandas Gandhi in India and Nelson Mandela in South Africa to the saints and the Prophets of God, those who are just not only suffer, but seem at times to suffer in direct proportion to their innocence and purity of heart.

Kim is a Christian. She and I had many conversations about the suffering of Christ. Many times I pointed out to her that He suffered brutally, that He was betrayed by His closest friends, publicly mocked and blamed, and finally crucified. "And did He deserve it?"

I would ask her. "No," she would answer. "No, of course not." And this paradox of life would hang in the room, beckoning her to open her heart to the possibilities that awaited her within a relationship with God. Kim gradually came to understand that if even the good Lord Himself were caused to suffer unjustly, and He was perfect, well, then maybe, just maybe, her own suffering was not her fault.

# You Are Important

*One of the most powerful and healing messages that comes from the world of religious belief and faith is that each person on earth is important, unique, and valuable.*

Unfortunately, too many who have suffered trauma like Kim and Marla have lost their sense of their intrinsic worth. Their own internal negative voice joins the chorus of the world to tell them, "It's your own fault that you are having problems." The voice of religious scripture tells us otherwise. I am reminded of a story about a woman I worked with a few years ago whose own sense of self-worth was about as low as it could be. She, too, had a history of childhood neglect and abandonment. Believe it or not, she was "cured" simply by reading a scriptural verse over and over again and truly taking it to heart. I will call this woman Tanisha.

Tanisha was thirty-two when she first came to see me. She had a son aged eight. She was a stay-at-home-mom and had been happy about it until about a year before I met her. At that time her husband of ten years had simply packed up and left—no note, no warning, and no alimony or child support, either. He took off, leaving Tanisha and her son high and dry. This sudden and dramatic turn of events in Tanisha's life had sent her reeling. She was losing weight, and she could barely sleep. She was frightened, depressed, and hopeless. She had begun reaching out to men and had formed a handful of intense, short-lived relationships, looking for someone to rescue her from her plight. The men she picked only hurt her more. None were good candidates for a steady, committed relationship. One was a drug dealer, one was already married, and one had a problem with keeping a steady job. He also had a drinking problem. As these relationships turned sour, Tanisha's sense of panic grew.

When I met Tanisha at our first psychotherapy session, I emphasized that she had every right to feel afraid but that I was sure she had inside her the resources to cope with the situation. I assured her that, even though she was still in a state of shock and confusion from the trauma, she could, over time, stand on her own two feet and be the mother her son needed. I urged her to look inside herself for her own internal resources rather than looking outside herself for someone to rescue her. She said she felt like she was drowning in the sea and just grabbing at men like a drowning person grabs at passing debris just to stay afloat. During our fourth session together, as part of our work on these themes, I wrote one of my favorite passages from scripture on a piece of paper and gave it to her. The passage read, "Dost thou reckon thyself only a puny form/ When within thee the universe is folded?"[13] Unfortunately, soon after this session, Tanisha suddenly dropped out of therapy. I took it as a bad sign, but I was proven wrong.

About a year and a half later, I heard from Tanisha again. She called on the telephone to tell me that she had found a great job, had ended all of her dysfunctional relationships, and was raising her son and working on a college degree.

"Good heavens!" I said. "Did you get into counseling with someone else after you left me, or what?" (I was secretly thinking she must have gone out and found a really *good* therapist!)

"No," she said. "I just kept reading that quote you gave me."

"Uh," I stammered, "what quote?"

"The quote about not being puny and having the whole universe inside me. I kept it on my refrigerator. I'm looking at it now. It's hanging right beside the serenity prayer and in between a picture of my son and a recipe for pumpkin pie. When my friends come in and read it, they always say, 'What's that? What does that mean?' I usually tell them that a friend gave it to me and it means that I am important."

"Well, you *are* important!" I exclaimed. "I am so proud of you! I'm amazed at what you have achieved!"

"Well," she said, "I remembered what you told me. You told me I was important and that I just needed some time to heal. You were the only one that I didn't feel was blaming me and judging me. I could tell you believed in me. After a while, I began to believe in myself."

# God as a Process

How do we explain this woman's amazing progress? Can we simply dismiss her explanation as foolishness? Or, might there be something more to it, something that science is only recently coming to understand about the power of the spirit to transform the body, the mind, and the emotions?

The newest views of science tell us that the universe, like the brain, is not so much a thing as it is a huge, cosmic, process. The universe is alive. Earth itself is alive. Creation is at all times in the ongoing process of creating itself and of "unfolding," as the quote says. You are part of this process.

*You are growing, developing, and unfolding your potential. The spiritual forces of life that animate all created things are within you, just as they are in the flowers, the rocks, and plants, and the saints, each according to its station and each according to its capacity.*

The religious traditions of the world give various names and labels to the animating spirit of the universe: God, Alláh, Jehovah, the Great Spirit, Brahman, the Tao, Ahura Mazda. These religious traditions as well as other spiritual disciplines tell us that we can directly connect ourselves to the animating spirit of the universe. The traditions tell us that doing so will have a healing, balancing, restorative effect upon us. Let's take a look at that idea and see if the concepts we have been applying to relationships among human beings may also apply to a relationship with God. Is it possible that you can change your neural templates by praying? Is it possible to attune to God? Does attunement to God have a healing effect?

# Growing Your Brain through Prayer

Answers to some of these questions are addressed in a fascinating book entitled *Why God Won't Go Away: Brain Science and the Biology of Belief.* The book is the result of a burgeoning area of research known as "neurotheology," or the study of the relationship between spirituality and the brain. In this book, authors Andrew Newberg, Eugene D'Aquili, and Vincent Rause present their understanding of the neurobiology of what they call peak meditative experiences. Their ingenious research methodology shows that meditators from various cultures and religious traditions experience similar brain changes during peak meditative experiences. The authors were able to demonstrate this fact by studying individuals in the process of meditation.

Their research design was ingenious. The authors report on studies of both Buddhist monks and Catholic nuns involved in the process of deep meditative prayer. Before the meditation began, the participants had an intravenous line placed in the vein of one arm. The line was ready for an injection of harmless radioactive material at the proper moment. The meditators each had a small string tied to one finger. They were told to tug on the string at the point when they reached the peak of their meditative experience. When the experimenters felt the tug, they injected the radioactive chemical into the subject. This chemical acted as a "tracer" of blood flow for a SPECT (Single Photon Emission Computed Tomography) scanner.

The authors reported similar findings among all the meditators they studied. During the peak periods of meditation a very specific area in the back of the brain was affected. The authors refer to this area as the OAA, or orientation association area. This part of the brain is usually associated with orienting the individual in physical space. It is associated with making the distinction between you (over here) and "not you," or the rest of the world (over there). Before meditation, this area of the meditators' brains was very active in helping to orient them in space and to distinguish between themselves and other things in the world. During the point of deepest meditation, however, blood flow to this part of the brain was greatly reduced. Interestingly, the meditators described this peak state of meditation as an experience of being "one" with the universe, of being united with all and content with all. They also reported a sense of being freed from the constraints of time and space. The authors refer to this state of consciousness as a mystical experience of "Absolute Unitary Being." The authors have explored whether or not this phenomenon might be an artifact of the mind, a symptom of illness, or a distortion of reality. They have concluded that it is none of these. They believe that the brain has the capacity to allow it to have an experience of relationship with the Absolute, or God. They say,

*"Mystical experiences . . . are not about magic, or mind-reading, or the conjuring of visions or spirits; it is nothing more or less than an uplifting sense of genuine spiritual union with something larger than the self."* [14]

# Health Benefits of Attunement to God

The similarity between the meditative state described in *Why God Won't Go Away* and the attunement process we have described is striking. The process involves turning attention to God to form a connection, or relationship, with God, attempting to attune to Him, and sustaining this state of prolonged attention and concentration for a period of time. Research suggests that this practice is good for you—not merely good for your spirit, but good for your mind and body as well. The authors say, "Studies have shown that men and women who practice any mainstream faith live longer, have fewer strokes, less heart disease, better immune system function, and lower blood pressure than the population at large. So impressive are the health benefits of religion, in fact, that after reviewing more than a thousand studies on the impact of religion upon health, Dr. Harold Koenig of Duke University Medical Center recently told *The New Republic* that

> *"Lack of religious involvement has an effect on mortality that is equivalent to forty years of smoking one pack of cigarettes per day."* [15]

The health benefits of spirituality have also been studied by Dr. Jared Kass, a psychologist who has developed several self-tests to measure the effect of spirituality on a person's life. The self-tests have proven so effective that they have been adopted by the U.S. Army. In an introduction to two of these self-tests, Dr. Kass writes, "In studies at Harvard and other centers, the following . . . tests have shown how tapping into your spiritual core can boost self-confidence, lower heart attack risk factors, reduce cravings for alcohol, and help stop smoking."[16]

My own religious beliefs are grounded in the Bahá'í Faith, to which I belong. The Bahá'ís believe in the fundamental unity of all religions. For me this belief means that I can join fully and authentically with those I work with and encourage them to embrace their own spiritual pathways as they go forward on the healing journey. I can help them step aside from the doctrinal divisions that sometimes distract the followers of various religions from the consistent and unfailing healing message that runs through all of the world's religions. God has not abandoned us. We are part of His creation, and we belong here. We all have a purpose in life. God loves us deeply, even if no one else on the planet seems to love us.

## Kim's Attunement to God

This message and the comfort and support it gave Kim were crucial to her healing and well-being. Kim's healing journey began when she made the decision to seek psychotherapy, and through her work with me, she has accomplished amazing things. However, she also attributes a great deal of her growth to her relationship with God. I will let her tell her story in her own words:

> *I must have believed in God as a kid, because I remember crying to God at night to just let me die. I figured He hated me like everyone else did and that's why He didn't let me die. I had to live as punish-*

*ment for being bad. That's how I saw it. I never went to church or anything, and God was never mentioned in my house. I do remember, one or two summers, going to Bible school with my cousin because I wanted to make the crafts that she was making. Other than that, I had no thoughts about God. When I got married we were married by the mayor, so that didn't even take place in a church.*

*When I joined a twelve-step program, they talked a lot about God. They said I had to pray even if I didn't believe in it. I couldn't. For many reasons, I saw it as a weakness. "All my life I took care of myself and never needed anyone," is what I thought. I also was sure that God didn't want to hear from me. I thought that my life was a punishment for being "born bad," that God would never do anything for me. I didn't feel I deserved God. I thought I had messed up somehow, and that's why God didn't like me. I couldn't even try to pray—until I was in enough pain, as a last resort.*

*I had been going to twelve-step meetings every day, and on weekends twice a day, for a couple of months, and it was getting harder and harder each time. I was so afraid. I couldn't stand being noticed. I was sure that when people looked at me they could see how repulsive I was. All I could focus on at the meetings was how uncomfortable I was. It got to the point that I couldn't go to meetings anymore. It was too painful. I also knew I couldn't live like this anymore. I didn't know what to do. I got on my knees and cried, "God please help me." That's all I knew to say. I hoped He would hear me. I didn't know what I needed, but I knew that my only other option was suicide. I couldn't stand being anymore. I hated myself so much.*

*Somehow I managed to keep going to meetings. I didn't all of a sudden have this great relationship with God or anything. I tried to believe. It was hard. I always had to see something to believe it. Now*

*I was told I had to believe in God and believe that He loved me. In fact, I often did not pray. When I did, I wasn't sure that God heard me, or that there even was a God. I guess I kind of looked at God as someone to call on when I couldn't handle something. Then I would pray and hope there was a God and that He would help me. Again, I didn't change anything until I was in enough pain. Apparently, pain motivates me.*

*At first, after the suicide attempt in early 1991, Dr. Pat sometimes talked of God. I wasn't ready to hear what she had to say. I was still too focused on how horrible I felt all the time to hear. But after some time, we began to talk about God. Once she told me that God is the only thing that can fill the void I felt deep inside me. She also reminded me to say my prayers every night. At first I would tell her I was praying when I really wasn't. I still didn't feel worthy of anything good like God. And I still believed I controlled my universe. I still believed that only I could take care of myself. I still believed I didn't need anything or anyone. I still saw it as a weakness. Eventually, I hurt enough to try to pray, but after I prayed I still wasn't sure about why I was praying. I still wasn't sure that my prayers would be answered. I still wasn't sure how to pray. Sometimes I would just tell God that I didn't know why I was praying, or what I needed. I just knew I needed help. I still hardly ever felt good. I was trying to pray, but still was not connecting. I was just saying words, hoping there was a God that would help me. Until I became desperate.*

*A friend of mine in the twelve-step program invited me to her church. It was a big, old, beautiful stone building. The inside was all gorgeous wood, all polished to perfection, with shining, colorful stained glass. It felt holy. The next Sunday I went back to that church even though my friend wasn't going. After the service, everyone left,* but I couldn't. I couldn't stop crying. I heard some people downstairs, but I don't even know if I was alone in the sanctuary. I couldn't even raise my head. I felt ashamed at being me and being in this beautiful, holy place. I felt ashamed at my inability to be around people. I felt ashamed of my past, and I didn't believe the future to be anything but dismal. I didn't deserve anything good. I just sobbed. Eventually, I heard someone sit in the pew in front of me. It was the pastor. She asked me if I was okay, or if she could do anything, or something like that. I don't remember exactly what. I do remember saying, "I'm trying to decide if I want to live or die." I have no recollection of the rest of my time at the church that day. I believe we talked for hours, even though I don't think I looked at her other than maybe a glance. I was still early in therapy and full of shame.

The pastor invited me back the next day, and I think I was sitting there waiting for her when she arrived at the church the next morning. She would let me sit up in the sanctuary and then come up and talk to me. Early on, before I left for the day, she would pray for me. I felt safe in there with her for some reason. She and Dr. Pat were the first people I remember who talked to me and wanted me to talk. I didn't under-stand that. I couldn't figure out why they wanted to listen to me. It kind of confused me. I so wanted to feel what being with them made me feel, but I was also filled with fear. Afraid of what I was feeling. Afraid to trust them. Afraid that after a while they would hate me and hurt me, too. The pastor and Dr. Pat were trying to convince me that I was worthy of God's love and that He did love me.

I don't know how long I went on meeting with the pastor. Every other day, it seemed. I know it was almost as often as I was seeing Dr. Pat. I'm not even sure what we talked about besides God. I think I told her about what a horrible mother I was for giving up my daugh-

*ter, and I think I told her about some of my past sexual abuses. I don't remember much of what she said. Mostly, I cried a lot and tried to find a reason for living, and I think she tried to help me find that reason. . . . I could see no reason for my life. During that time it felt like I was hanging on by my fingernails. Trying so hard to want to live.*

*I spent a lot of time talking with the pastor and Dr. Pat about God, but I felt so bad, I don't think I heard much. I was in so much pain, that's all I could focus on. The pastor continued to let me sit in the sanctuary, almost whenever I felt like it, and eventually came up and sat with me. One day when she came up to see me I was on the balcony. She came up and found the noose I had made. She rightly became angry and untied the noose. I don't remember anything else, like what was said. I do know that that was most likely the lowest point of my life. It was as if I were standing on the edge of a cliff, left with the decision of which way to turn. I felt so ashamed that I had done that to her, and I still could not grab on to a reason for living. I believe it was at that point that I gave up and let God help me. It's not a decision I made, and I didn't feel anything. I think I just gave up and stopped fighting God. I don't really know what happened. I only know that from that day on, I really tried to find a God of my own.*

*It took years for me to find a concept of God that I felt comfortable with. I learned that my original concept of God portrayed Him as a puppeteer controlling what we did here on earth. I did not take into account His gift of free will. I didn't see that all the bad things that happened were manmade, not God-made. I also learned that I was judging the people who went to church, pointing out that they were sinners, thinking of all the people I knew who claimed to worship*

God that were complete jerks. I learned to not care what other people did. That was between them and God, not me. The hardest thing I had to learn to believe was that God loved even me. That took me a long time.

Sometime in this spiritual journey, I did have another unsuccessful suicide attempt. I was extremely depressed and collected a hose and some duct tape to kill myself with my car exhaust. I originally parked in a cemetery, seeing that as fitting. Unfortunately, it was all open space, and I feared getting caught, so I disconnected the hose and rode around some more. I eventually parked in the middle of a Christmas tree farm. I assumed I would just go to sleep. It didn't turn out that way. I was sitting in the car, having trouble breathing, my mouth and nose extremely dry. I tried leaving the car running for only a short time, shutting it off, starting it again, etc. I eventually unhooked the hose again, went to a convenience store for a soda, and went back to the farm to try again. I lasted a little longer this time, but I finally did have to give up. I didn't just go to sleep like I expected to.

I was gone a couple of days trying to decide what to do but eventually parked in the church parking lot. The pastor and my friend convinced me to go to the hospital. I spent at least a month there. I felt much better when I came out. Thank God Dr. Pat and the pastor both forgave me. I really hate to think what it would have done to me if they hadn't. I was very fragile (for years, and quite often I still am). I was grateful to be out of the hospital and ready to start over. I began attending church every week, and the pastor invited me to get involved. I began helping out with the children's Sunday school. It was very hard at first, because I still could not relax around adults. Give me a bunch of kids alone, by myself, and I'm fine, but when an

adult is around to view the interaction I cannot be myself. I was
eventually able to relax a little and become fairly comfortable.

I began to change. I loved Sunday's church service (particularly
the singing . . . ). I learned how to pray. I noticed that now when I
prayed, I didn't "hope" He answered my prayers, I "knew" He would.
I learned that God loves me, just because He's God. I used to think I
had to earn God's love. I tried to be good my whole life, thinking if
I was good enough my family would love me. Now I try to be very
good for different reasons. It's out of gratitude. I try to do the right
things because I'm so grateful to God. The pastor once said to me,
"God gives us minimum protection but maximum support." I needed
to hear that. I know God cannot protect me from people or life, but
He is with me all the time. I don't pray for things anymore. That's
asking for my will. Mostly I pray for gratitude, strength and courage,
love, the ability to be a good Christian, complete trust and faith in
Him, and knowledge of His will for me. I learned over time to feel
God with me.

. . . As I became closer to God I felt better. I began to feel that
maybe there was a purpose for my life, even if that purpose is just to
be an example of God's grace. I never felt there was a reason for my
life before. Then, in January of 2000, I was sexually assaulted by a
stranger in my home. By this time I was getting better at feeling
things, and this one hurt like hell. I was full of pain, mostly shame.
Over the next couple of months I would try to pray but end up
cursing God and telling Him I hated Him. I couldn't believe this
could happen again. How could God let that happen again? Inside I
knew God didn't make this happen, but I guess I needed somewhere
for my anger to go. I was in a lot of pain, and I was scared. I was
afraid I would never feel close to God again.

*I don't know what got me through those months when all I wanted was to die. I remember the pastor reminding me that God was probably crying, too. That helped somehow. Then, on Mother's Day, I went on a weekend retreat at a Catholic retreat house in Pennsylvania. While there, I signed up to have a one-on-one talk with one of the nuns. I told her about my fears. She interpreted my anger at God as another form of prayer. And she also made me feel better when she said, "Don't we get angry at the people we're closest to?" That made me feel less guilty about yelling at God. It also gave me hope that I could get back the relationship I had had with God before this happened. God never left me. I left God.*

*It has taken a long time for me to recover. Thank God I had the foundation I had before this happened. Even when I was at my lowest, wishing I could die, and sitting in parking lots at bars trying to get up the courage to go in, I still deep inside felt God just enough to keep me going. Interestingly, the hardest things to go through have brought me closer to God. I could no more live without God than I could live without air. I know I am nothing without God, but with God I can be anything I want to be. Rather than a weakness, relying on God has been my chief source of strength. I'm not one to believe that everything happens for a reason. To me, that sounds like everything is preplanned, like God makes things happen. I can't believe God thought, "Kim has to learn a lesson. I'll have her get raped." I do believe that everything that happens can be a learning experience if I keep my mind open. And I am sure that, no matter what happens, God is with me in it, giving me strength and courage to get through.*

*Life is just life, very good sometimes, and very bad sometimes. Without God, it would all mean nothing to me, like it did before. My prayers are very simple now. First I thank Him for all the bless-*

*ings He's given me, particularly the people He's put in my life. Then I ask Him to help me face each moment and each person of this day with love and gratitude. I ask Him to take my will from me and give me the knowledge of, and the strength and courage to carry out, His will for me. I ask Him to forgive me my sins and help me to become a better Christian. I ask Him to help me to have complete trust and faith in Him so that I won't be so afraid anymore, and so I won't worry so much about money, my job, my illness, my lack of ability to have close relationships, etc. . . . . And I ask Him to help me learn to give and receive love. I ask Him to help me heal. Then I usually say my favorite prayer:*

*Thou hast given so much to me, give one thing more . . .*

*A grateful heart.*

*Not thankful when it pleases me as if thy blessings have spare days . . .*

*But such a heart whose pulse may be*

*Thy Praise.*

—Anonymous

## Summary

Kim's story traces her spiritual path from feeling alone in the universe, with only herself to blame for all of her troubles, to feeling compassion for herself, relying upon God, and feeling one with the universe. When Kim began her spiritual journey, she believed that she—not God—controlled her universe. She believed that she could and should take care of herself and that to do otherwise was a sign of weakness. As she came into contact with those to whom she turned for help—her friends in the twelve-step program, her pastor, and me—she was repeatedly advised to turn to God and "pay attention" to Him.

At first, she resisted, only turning to God when she was desperate, merely "hoping" and not really believing that God would hear her prayers. Eventually she became desperate, broke down while praying in church, and decided to "stop fighting God." She describes this moment as "the lowest point" in her life. She felt as if she were "standing on the edge of a cliff, left with the decision of which way to turn." At that point she gave up and let God help her. From that day forward, she began making a conscious effort to feel a connection with God. Her pastor told her,

> *"God gives minimum protection but*
> *maximum support."*

Something about that statement resonated inside Kim. She began to commune more fully with God and started to feel herself changing. She was finally able to feel the mutual flow of relationship between herself and God and began to relax and feel safe. She developed a relationship with God, a God with Whom she can even be angry when tragedy strikes once again, confident that He is always there for her.

Kim's pattern of movement toward God brings to mind the processes of attunement and attachment as described in chapters 2 and 3. At first, Kim was not attuned to God and had a "disorganized and disoriented" attachment to Him. She did not feel that God provided a "secure base" for her. However, as her spiritual journey unfolded, she began to attune and learned how to get "in sync" with God. As her attachment to God grew, she began to turn to Him not only in times of trouble but also when things were going well.

Over time she developed a complete reliance upon God. Her attachment to Him became secure. Today she feels loved and cared for by God and moves through life with meaning and purpose, knowing that she has an important role to play, feeling deeply connected with all that there is. She has found her true spiritual self, and with that discovery have come the twin fruits of purpose and gratitude. These flow back and forth within her and flow out into the world in the form of service to others.

# Chapter 7

# It's Not Your Fault

THE TITLE OF THIS BOOK READS, "It's Not Your Fault." What is it, exactly, that is not your fault? First and foremost,

> *If negative experiences have left you a legacy*
> *of emotional pain or distress, it is not your fault.*
> *It is not your fault that these experiences happened*
> *to you. Nor is it your fault that you continue to*
> *feel pain even after the events are over.*

It is impossible to endure traumas such as childhood abandonment, neglect, physical abuse, sexual abuse, emotional abuse, and other traumas and losses without being hurt by these experiences. And it is not your fault if traumatic events have made a lasting impression on you.

Experiences of all kinds—both good and bad—change the way your brain works. Therefore, your way of thinking about yourself and the world is based on the way you have been treated. This is not your fault either; it is simply a fact of life. And it is not your fault that your desire to heal from your painful past is not sufficient in and of itself to effect healing.

*If you have been traumatized, you need help from
other people in order to heal. This is not the result
of a deficit or a weakness on your part, it is
the way the brain works.*

As you get the help you need, it will also not be your fault that the healing process will take time. You will be "growing your brain" and forming neural templates that will eventually allow you to relate to the world in new and better ways. It is also not your fault that bad things happen in the world and that some of these bad things have happened to you. Being a recipient of the world's injustice is not the same as causing or inviting the injustice. We established in chapter 1 that your brain is not like a computer. You can't just flip a switch and shift to a new program. No, you are a part of nature. You grow and develop the way nature does—organically, in stages, within a context of relationships with other living things.

# General Principles of the Healing Journey

The book's subtitle reads, "How Healing Relationships Change Your Brain and Can Help You Overcome a Painful Past." We have seen through the story of Kim how relationships can bring about healing. By looking closely at her healing process, we have examined several important principles of the healing journey.

First, Kim integrated many approaches and accepted the help of many people in her healing process. She did not narrow her focus to only one area of concern or one type of intervention. For example, she addressed her mental illness by consulting a physician and taking medication as prescribed. She accepted hospitalization when necessary. She became involved in a twelve-step program and stayed involved in order to overcome her addiction to alcohol and drugs. She used psychotherapy with me to overcome her problems resulting from past traumas, including all the complex issues we discussed in chapter 5. She relied on her spiritual life to give her the inner strength to carry the journey forward even when the obstacles in her path seemed almost insurmountable. The synergy created by this combination of different approaches gave Kim a lot of positive momentum. She literally filled her life with people who supported her and with experiences that were healthy, positive, and encouraging.

Second, during our sessions together and through her own study and reading, Kim became educated about the science of emotional development, relationship experiences, and the biological realities of trauma. She learned about how and why biology and experience had interacted to cause her pain and suffering. Through this education, Kim developed a compassionate understanding of herself that enabled her to acknowledge and then let go of her past. Her new understanding enabled her to stop seeing herself as a worthless person who was made wrong from the start and to begin viewing herself as the heroine of her life's story.

Third, Kim obtained support from me in a positive, long-term, attuned relationship. My consistently positive view of her provided the new experience of a relationship that would allow her to "grow her brain" and develop the secure emotional base that she needed. Within the context of our relationship she found the sense of safety and nurturing that she needed to explore her past of trauma and abuse. This secure relationship enabled her to develop deeper insight into herself and progressively greater degrees of emotional control and self-confidence.

Fourth, Kim integrated her spiritual life into her psychological healing process. She benefited from the marriage of science and religion. She found that the principles of compassion for self and service to others were logical, well-researched and supported spiritual truths. Her journal entries convey the fact that her spiritual understanding of herself was a key to her healing process. It remains the bedrock of her current sense of well-being and stability. Spiritual principles continue to guide her daily actions. Compassion has replaced anger and self-loathing. Understanding has replaced judgment and self-condemnation. And service to others has replaced her formerly self-destructive behavior.

## The Power of Relationship

We see that all four of the main principles of healing that Kim employed involved relationships with others. From the medical community to the church community, from her individual therapist to her twelve-step support groups, many people and relationships combined to help move Kim out of the darkness of hopelessness and depressed self-loathing to become the spiritually vibrant and giving person she is today.

The previous chapters dramatically demonstrate that

*Our relationships with other human beings affect us in ways that are far more radical and direct than we might ever have thought possible.*

This is true not only for Kim but for all of us. The attunement process is a clear example. We have seen that through the eye-to-eye, face-to-face emotional connection between parents and children, nervous system templates are formed. The process occurs subtly, unconsciously, and without fanfare. To an outside observer, these attuned interchanges look like nothing at all, like a parent and a baby just doing what comes naturally. Yet, these interchanges are "brain-changing" and life-changing. What does this fact tell us about everyday life and the many interchanges with others that occur all day long? How are we affecting others? How are we being affected? The chapter on attachment expands on the central idea of the importance of relationships by illustrating how early attachments form the bedrock of our sense of self. Secure, caring, compassionate relationships become integrated into our sense of ourselves as people who are secure, caring, and compassionate. And in the trauma chapters, we saw the other side of that. We saw that when people are hurt by others they become ruled by fear and pain, which often comes out as rage and anger toward other people.

## The Web of Life

The preceding discussion raises interesting questions about our worldview and the responsibility of each of us, whether personally injured or not, to help heal the traumas of the past. The chapters in this book challenge popular myths prevalent in today's culture that liken human beings to little machine-like creatures chugging along, side-by-side but fundamentally isolated and disconnected from one another. When one of us "breaks down," the others chime in, "You need to get *yourself* together. Just do it. There is nothing *we* can do about *your* problems. *We* are separate from *you*. There is nothing really wrong with you anyway. It's just all in your head. Snap out of it, why don't you. Or do you just *want* to be sick?"

From this point of view of mechanistic isolation, individual responsibility can easily be narrowed to self-interest. From this vantage point, human beings can argue that the pain of others is not their problem, and from this unsympathetic stance it is only a short jump to blaming victims for their pain and implying that if they had only tried a little harder they could have somehow prevented their own injuries. These ideas are the unspoken attitudes and biases that the emotionally injured must battle every day.

Until recently, science seemed to support the mechanistic view. Now, new paradigms of science support the fundamental connectedness and unity of all of creation. This "new" science, as it is called, acknowledges that

> *Human beings are not isolated from each other*
> *but are fundamentally connected within a web*
> *of relationships with each other, with the*
> *environment, and with God.*

Each of us bears some responsibility to help and serve others, and each of us has the ability to gain strength and health through positive, direct connection with each other and with God.

From this new viewpoint, the Golden Rule—to "Do unto others as you would have them do unto you"—takes on a scientific as well as a spiritual significance. We are beginning to see science assert that fostering spirituality increases "resilience" even in army personnel.

We see that "social support" is a factor that increases health and reduces the negative effects of disease. And in the popular media, prayer and meditation have become "stress reducers" that increase longevity and boost the immune system's ability to fight off disease.

As a society we are coming to a scientific understanding of what spiritual traditions have taught for centuries—that human beings are not disconnected, solitary entities. On the contrary,

*Our very bodies, with their infinitely complicated and marvelous nervous systems, are set up for relationship connections with each other and with God.*

## Responsibility versus Blame and Intergenerational Transmission of Trauma

Does being connected with others mean that those who are injured can just sit back, relax, blame others, and somehow expect the world to make up for what has happened to them? Absolutely not. It is important to make a distinction between blame and responsibility. I have often said to people I work with,

*"Your problems are not your fault, but you are the only one who can solve them."*

You see, even though you are not to blame for the legacy of trauma and unresolved loss that may have been passed on to you from your parents' generation, the problems are now your responsibility. Why? Because of your children and your children's children and even because of the children next door and down the block. Each generation must bear responsibility for the health and welfare of the next generation.

On a societal level, discussions of how to limit the "ripple effect" of war and other traumatic events have only just begun. Our discussion has shown that children come into the world with immature nervous systems and completely underdeveloped emotional control systems. Their psychological health is dependent upon their relationships with others. As our culture becomes more and more permeated with unresolved trauma and loss, the legacies of war, crime, abuse, and other injuries, the children of the culture become traumatized by generation upon generation of unresolved issues.

*Each of us bears some responsibility to try*
*to heal the traumas of the past and*
*protect succeeding generations from*
*further traumatization.*

There are many ways we can do this. We can seek help if we need it ourselves, we can assist others who have been traumatized to find the help they need, we can educate ourselves to be the best parents we can be, and we can connect with God and allow Him to be a positive force in our lives.

And now, what about Kim?

# Epilogue

Kim currently lives with her daughter in her own home in a small town on the East Coast. She does not have contact with her former husband, who gave up his parental rights some time ago. Kim's relationship with her family of origin is uneven. She is close to some of her family members and estranged from others. One of her brothers has passed away. The brother who molested her moved far away, and she has not seen or spoken to him in twenty years. She has not confronted him, nor does she intend to do so. She has told her mother a little about her experiences, but she has not gone into detail. Her mother has apologized for not doing better, and she has since attempted to be supportive to Kim. Kim understands that when her father left home without making any financial provisions for the care of the family's ten children, her mother was traumatized. She did what she had to do to survive, and Kim has come to understand this and has made peace with her mother. Kim is very close to two of her sisters, who live in the same town and frequently share child care and other daily chores with her. Kim has not discussed her entire story with anyone either inside or outside the family. She has shared bits and pieces with people as she felt it was safe and appropriate. This is her choice.

Although Kim has made miraculous progress since the first time I saw her, her life is not perfect, and it is not without setbacks. She recently chose to go into a psychiatric hospital for a few days when she became severely depressed. This was her first hospitalization in about five years, and it came as a result of changing her work schedule from day shift to night shift. After about six months of working the night shift, she could no longer cope with being cut off from all of the supportive relationships in her twelve-step program. Fortunately, she was strong enough to be able to advocate for herself and landed a daytime position with the same company. She also returned to therapy for a time to begin working on her next big issue, which is intimate relationships with men.

This has been the most difficult area for Kim. She does not trust men. She has been afraid thus far to go through the dating and testing processes necessary to find a permanent partner. This is her next goal. She says she may reach it or she may not, but she is happy and content now, even without this companionship. She says that each day, she awakens and thanks God for her life and tries to keep an attitude of gratitude throughout the day.

As for me, the professional confusion I discussed in the introduction has largely quieted. I no longer experience a sense of conflict between my own spiritual values and beliefs and the dictates of science. I now confidently base my work with clients on an integration of neurobiology and development. I can barely talk to someone without drawing the brain and explaining something about how emotions work and what kinds of things cause problems. I keep attachment principles at the forefront of therapy and realize that those with insecure attachment styles may be quite anxious about forming a close bond and may be as resistant as Kim was at the beginning of our work. I keep in mind that it is my job to remain consistent, safe, and nurturing—the hallmarks of the attuned caregiver.

I am excited about new developments that each day shed more light on the amazing interaction between nature and nurture. The new understanding that these developments will bring to so many areas of human behavior is staggering. Neurobiology will be at the forefront as brain-behavior relationships become clearer. Someday, I hope to know that I am saying and doing the right things with clients because I will be able to see their brains changing in the right way! Until then, I will continue to follow new developments, especially those that integrate the spiritual with the psychological and neurobiological.

In addition to my work with individuals, I am attempting to share some of this important information about the effect of experiences on the brain with those who deal with children. From parents, to teachers, to those who run child welfare agencies and those who deal with children who break the law, everyone needs to know that children are dramatically affected by their relationship environment. Measures to ensure the safety and security of children are a paramount need in our society. Institutions from schools to hospitals and government programs need to understand and respect the power of intimate bonds.

# Summing Up

I have attempted to dispel some of the myths and misconceptions that people bring to the subject of healing from emotional wounds and replace them with an understanding of the healing power of relationships. I have explained that humans are not isolated, disconnected entities responsible only to themselves and impervious to others. Rather, I have shown that we all live together in a state of deep and profound connection that can be either mutually beneficial or mutually destructive. I have made a case for trying to empathize with those in pain and trying to imagine what it would be like to live in their shoes rather than shunning or blaming them. I have tried to show that helping others helps you, too, and that all of us depend on each other throughout our lives. I have tried to bring to your awareness the importance of how we treat children. I have discussed how impressionable their minds are at certain critical periods of life. I have attempted to be both scientifically sound and personally integrative. I have attempted to bridge science and religion, psychology and biology. I have attempted to make distinctions in a way that conveys the importance of "all things working together" to help those who have been hurt.

All of this I have tried to convey through the story of Kim by weaving her story in and out of the scientific information. In all arenas and by all accounts, I have taken great liberties with details in order to convey the "big picture" without becoming tedious. Many others have written in greater detail with a higher degree of scientific accuracy and rigor. Some of these people and their work are listed in the annotated bibliography at the end of the book. My hope is that you will read more and continue to expand your understanding as the science of trauma, the brain, and relationships develops in the future.

Overall, I hope you will find the discussion enlightening and personally empowering. I hope something in what I have said will help you attune more fully to yourself and to others in your life. As you go forward, if things get really tough, really difficult, remember Kim and her amazing story and take heart. Look around you for someone to help and support you, and while you do this, remember, life is not always kind or fair. If you are in pain, the fact may be that it's just not your fault.

# Notes

1. Matt Ridley, "What Makes You Who You Are" *Time* 161, no. 22 (June 2, 2003): 55–63.

2. John Bowlby, *Maternal Care and Mental Health*, quoted in John Bowlby, *A Secure Base: Parent-Child Attachment and Healthy Human Development*, p. 21.

3. Humberto Maturana and Francisco Varela, *The Tree of Life*, pp. 128–29.

4. See ibid., p. 129.

5. David Livingstone, quoted in Peter Levine and Ann Frederick, *Waking the Tiger*, pp. 136–37.

6. Peter Levine and Ann Frederick, *Waking the Tiger*, p. 138.

7. See Babette Rothchild, *The Body Remembers: The Psychophysiology of Trauma and Trauma Treatment* (New York: W. W. Norton, 2000).

8. Peter Levine and Ann Frederick, *Waking the Tiger*, p. 238.

9. Edna Foa, Terence Keane, and Matthew Friedman, *Effective Treatments for PTSD*, p. 370.

10. See Aphrodite Matsakis, *I Can't Get Over It*, pp. 113–40

11. See Melvin J. Lerner, *The Belief in a Just World: A Fundamental Delusion* (New York: Plenum Press, 1980).

12. Harold S. Kushner, *When Bad Things Happen to Good People* (New York: HarperCollins, 1981).

13. The Imam 'Alí, quoted in Bahá'u'lláh, *The Seven Valleys*, p. 34.

14. Andrew Newberg, et al., *Why God Won't Go Away: Brain Science and the Biology of Belief*, p. 129–30.

15. Ibid.

16. See www.spiritualityhealth.com/newsh/items/blank/item_3019.html; Jared Kass, "Two Tests Across Your Soul Body Connection," <http://www.spiritualityhealth.com/newsh/items/selftest/item_234.html>.

# Appendix 1

# How to Get Help

I HAVE ADVOCATED COMBINING MANY different approaches and resources during the healing process. Here are some suggestions about
how you can begin to find the help you need if you have been
traumatized.

It is usually best to begin your healing journey with a visit to
your family medical doctor. He or she will screen you for medical
issues and can provide you with referrals to appropriate resources
in your area, including psychiatrists, hospital-based programs, and
other medical treatments for mental illness, if needed. To find a
psychotherapist, ask your medical doctor for a referral, or look into
local community resources. These include community mental health
centers, which are available in most areas and are required by law to
provide mental health services on a sliding fee scale, according to
your income level.

Private practitioners in psychiatry, psychology, social work, and
related disciplines can often be found by looking in the telephone
book or by calling the respective state organizations and asking for
a referral. If you have private health insurance, you may wish to
call your insurance company to find out what your mental health
benefits are. Many insurance companies require certain procedures

to access your benefits. They may also have referral resources for you. If you are employed by an organization that has an employee assistance program, they can provide appropriate referrals. If a history of trauma is part of your problem, be sure to ask to be seen by someone with training and expertise in this area. I recommend that you interview prospective practitioners to find the one that is best for you. Reputable practitioners will not be offended if you interview them for this purpose.

To find self-help organizations that deal with addictions to alcohol, drugs, gambling, sex, eating disorders, or other problems, ask your family doctor for assistance, or look in your local telephone directory. Alcoholics Anonymous is one such organization that can help those who want to recover from alcoholism. Realize that you may need to attend a number of different groups to find the one that is best for you.

To find a local faith-based organization or church group that meets your needs, consult with friends, relatives, or some of the resources mentioned above. Some of these organizations offer support groups and other resources for those dealing with emotional difficulties.

These are only a few general suggestions. It is sometimes difficult to get started on the healing journey because energy and resourcefulness are needed at a time when they may be in very short supply. Try to persevere. Do not give up if your first attempts to find help are unsatisfactory. Often a search to find a "good fit" is necessary. Kim tried many different approaches before she settled into the treatment regimen described in the text. Keep trying, and don't get discouraged. If you wish, you may contact me at my Web site at http://www.trauma-recovery.com.

# Appendix 2

# A Word to the Professionals

AFTER HEARING MY LECTURES, many professionals who work in fields related to trauma and emotional healing often ask how to pursue the ideas of this book in greater depth. Many sources of information are available. I will mention here only a few of the books and resources that I found particularly useful as I wrote this book.

Daniel J. Siegel's *The Developing Mind: How Relationships and the Brain Interact to Shape Who We Are* is an excellent professional treatment of most of the ideas presented here, with the exception of those that deal with spirituality. To understand the brain and how it functions, I relied upon Antonio Damasio's highly praised book, *The Feeling of What Happens: Body and Emotion in the Making of Consciousness*. Maturana, Humberto, and Varela's *The Tree of Knowledge: The Biological Roots of Human Understanding* is also very thought-provoking and informative. For a neurobiological understanding of emotional development, including attunement and an application of these ideas to psychoanalytic theory, see Allan Schore's book *Affect Regulation and the Origin of the Self: The Neurobiology of Emotional Development*.

Much has been written on the subject of attachment. I found all of John Bowlby's works to be useful and readable, from his original work, *Attachment,* to his more recent *A Secure Base: Parent-Child Attachment and Healthy Human Development.*

To get a better understanding of the impact of spirituality on healing, I recommend the work of Herbert Benson, including his books *The Relaxation Response* and *Beyond the Relaxation Response.* For more information, visit the Mind Body Institute's Web site at http://www.mbmi.org.

For those who are interested in learning more about trauma, Bessel van der Kolk's books and articles are essential. Van der Kolk's work is often presented at annual meetings of the International Society for Traumatic Stress Studies (http://www.istss.org). The ISTSS publishes the *Journal of Traumatic Stress,* an excellent source of information on trauma and treatment. Another organization that holds excellent annual meetings is the International Society for the Study of Dissociation (http://www.issd.org). The society publishes the *Journal of Trauma and Dissociation.*

For those interested in learning more about EMDR, information is available from the EMDR Institute (http://www.emdr.com).

I welcome questions and comments from other professionals. You may reach me at my Web site: http://www.trauma-recovery.com.

# Bibliography

American Psychiatric Association. *Diagnostic and Statistical Manual of Mental Disorders*. Washington, DC: American Psychiatric Association, 1994.

Bahá'u'lláh, *The Seven Valleys*. New ed. Translated by Marzieh Gail and Ali-Kuli Khan. Wilmette, Ill.: Bahá'í Publishing Trust, 1991.

Benson, Herbert, with Miriam Z. Klipper. *The Relaxation Response*. 25th ed. New York: Avon, 2000.

Benson, Herbert, with William Proctor. *Beyond the Relaxation Response: How to Harness the Healing Power of Your Personal Beliefs*. New York: Berkley, 1984.

Bloom, Sandra. *Creating Sanctuary: Toward an Evolution of Sane Societies*. New York: Routledge, 1997.

Bowlby, John. *Attachment*. New York: Basic Books, 1982.

———. *Maternal Care and Mental Health*. New York: Columbia University Press, 1951.

———. *A Secure Base: Parent-Child Attachment and Healthy Human Development*. London: Routledge, 1988.

Capra, Fritjof. *The Hidden Connections: Integrating the Biological, Cognitive, and Social Dimensions of Life into a Science of Sustainability*. New York: Doubleday, 2002.

———. *The Web of Life: A New Scientific Understanding of Living Systems*. New York: Anchor Books, 1996.

Cassidy, Jude, and Phillip Shaver, eds. *Handbook of Attachment: Theory, Research, and Clinical Applications*. New York: Guilford Press, 2002.

Chu, James. *Rebuilding Shattered Lives: The Responsible Treatment of Complex Post-Traumatic and Dissociative Disorders*. New York: John Wiley, 1998.

Damasio, Antonio. *Descartes' Error: Emotion, Reason, and the Human Brain*. New York: Avon, 1995.

———. *The Feeling of What Happens: Body and Emotion in the Making of Consciousness*. New York: Harcourt, 1999.

Everly, George, Jr., and Jeffrey Lating, eds. *Psychotraumatology: Key Papers and Care Concepts in Post-Traumatic Stress.* New York: Plenum Press, 1995.

Foa, Edna, Terence Keane, and Matthew Friendman, eds. *Effective Treatment for PTSD: Practice Guidelines from the International Society for Traumatic Stress Studies.* New York: Guilford Press, 2000.

Herman, Judith. *Trauma and Recovery: The Aftermath of Violence—From Domestic Abuse to Political Terror.* New York: Basic Books, 1997.

Jordan, Judith, Alexandra Kaplan, Jean Miller, Irene Stiver, and Janet Surrey. *Women's Growth in Connection: Writings from the Stone Center.* New York: Guilford Press, 1991.

Kalb, Claudia. "Faith and Healing." *Newsweek,* November 10, 2003, 44–56.

Kirkpatrick, Lee. "Attachment and Religious Representations and Behavior." In Cassidy, Jude, and Phillip Shaver, eds. *Handbook of Attachment: Theory, Research, and Clinical Applications,* 803. New York: Guilford Press, 2002.

Kushner, Harold. *When Bad Things Happen to Good People.* New York: HarperCollins, 1981.

Larson, David, and Dale Matthews. "Spirituality and Medical Outcomes." Paper presented at *Spirituality & Healing in Medicine,* Boston, December 3–5, 1995.

Larson, D. B., E. M. Pattison, D. G. Blazer, et al. "The Measurement of Religion in Psychiatric Research." *Psychiatry and Religion: Overlapping Concerns.* Edited by L. H. Robinson. Washington, D.C.: APA Press, 1986, 155–77.

LeDoux, Joseph. *The Emotional Brain: The Mysterious Underpinnings of Emotional Life.* New York: Simon and Schuster, 1996.

Lemonick, Michael. "How Your Mind Can Heal Your Body." *Time,* January 20, 2003, 62–69.

Lerner, Melvin. *The Belief in a Just World: A Fundamental Delusion (Perspectives in Social Psychology Series).* New York: Plenum Press, 1980.

Levine, Peter. "Working with the Body to Resolve Trauma." Paper presented at the conference "Psychological Trauma: Maturational Processes and Therapeutic Interventions," Boston, March 23–24, 2001.

Levine, Peter, and Ann Frederick (contributor). *Waking the Tiger, Healing the Trauma: The Innate Capacity to Transform Overwhelming Experiences.* Berkeley: North Atlantic Books, 1997.

Lyons-Ruth, Karlen. "The Relational Context of Trauma: Fear, Dissociation, and Disorganized Early Attachment Relationships." Paper presented at the conference "Psychological Trauma: Maturational Processes and Therapeutic Interventions," Boston, March 23–24, 2001.

Lyons-Ruth, Karlen, and Deborah Jacobvitz. "Attachment Disorganization: Unresolved Loss, Relational Violence, and Lapses in Behavioral and Attentional Strategies." In J. Cassidy and P. Shaver (Eds.), *Handbook of Attachment: Theory, Research, and Clinical Implications,* 520–54. New York: Guilford, 1999.

Matsakis, Aphrodite. *I Can't Get Over It: A Handbook for Trauma Survivors.* Oakland, CA: New Harbinger Publications, 1996.

Maturana, Humberto, and Francisco Varela. *The Tree of Knowledge: The Biological Roots of Human Understanding.* Boston: Shambhala Publications, 1998.

Miller, Jean. *Toward a New Psychology of Women.* 2nd ed. Boston: Beacon Press, 1987.

Nathanson, Donald. *Shame and Pride: Affect, Sex, and the Birth of the Self.* New York: W. W. Norton, 1992.

Newberg, Andrew, Eugene D'Aquili, and Vince Rause. *Why God Won't Go Away: Brain Science and the Biology of Belief.* New York: The Ballantine Publishing Group, 2002.

Palmer, Louise. "Spirituality Becomes 'Resilience' and Joins the U.S. Army." *Spirituality and Health,* December 2003.

Pelcovitz, David, Bessel van der Kolk, Susan Roth, Francine Mandel, Sandra Kaplan, Patricia Resick. "Development of a Criteria Set and a Structured Interview for Disorders of Extreme Stress (SIDES)." *Journal of Traumatic Stress* 10 (1997): 1.

Pert, Candace B., *Molecules of Emotion: The Science behind Mind-Body Medicine*. New York: Touchstone, 1997.

Ridley, Matt. "What Makes You Who You Are." *Time,* June 2, 2003, 54–63.

Rothschild, Babette. *The Body Remembers: The Psychophysiology of Trauma and Trauma Treatment*. New York: W. W. Norton, 2000.

Schore, Allan. *Affect Regulation and the Origin of the Self: The Neurobiology of Emotional Development*. Mahwah, NJ: Lawrence Erlbaum Associates, 1999.

———. "The Neural Biology of Attachment and the Origin of Self: Implications for Theory and Clinical Practice." Paper presented on September 8, at the Eye Movement Desensitization Reprocessing Conference, Toronto, September 8–September 10, 2000.

Shapiro, Francine. *Eye Movement Desensitization and Reprocessing: Basic Principles, Protocols, and Procedures*. New York: Guilford Press, 2001.

Shalev, Arieh, Rachel Yehuda, and Alexander McFarlane, eds. *International Handbook of Human Response to Trauma*. New York: Kluwer Academic / Plenum Press, 2000.

Siegel, Daniel. *The Developing Mind: How Relationships and the Brain Interact to Shape Who We Are*. New York: Guilford Press, 2001.

Slade, Arietta. "Attachment Theory and Research: Implications for the Theory and Practice of Individual Psychotherapy with Adults." In Cassidy, Jude, and Phillip Shaver, eds. *Handbook of Attachment: Theory, Research, and Clinical Applications,* 575. New York: Guilford Press, 2002.

Solomon, Judith, and Carol George, eds. *Attachment Disorganization*. New York: Guilford Press, 1999.

Steinberg, Marlene, and Maxine Schnall. *The Stranger in the Mirror*. New York: Quill, 2001.

Van der Kolk, Bessel. "The Body Keeps the Score." *Harvard Review of Psychiatry* 1 (1994): 253–65.

———. "Neurobiology, Attachment and Trauma." Presentation given at the annual meeting of the International Society for Traumatic Stress Studies, Washington, DC, November 1998.

———. *Psychological Trauma*. Washington, DC: American Psychiatric Press, 1987.

Van der Kolk, Bessel, Alexander McFarlane, and Lars Weisaeth. *Traumatic Stress: The Effects of Overwhelming Experience on Mind, Body, and Society*. New York: Guilford Press, 1996.

Van der Kolk, Bessel, David Pelcovitz, Susan Roth, Francine Mandel, Alexander McFarlane, Judith Herman. "Dissociation, Somatization, and Affect Dysregulation: The Complexity of Adaptation to Trauma." *American Journal of Psychiatry* 153 (July 1996): 7, Festschrift Supplement.

Wahlberg, L., Bessel van der Kolk, E. Brett, and C. Marmar. *PTSD: Anxiety Disorder or Dissociative Disorder?* Symposium at the annual meeting of the International Society for Traumatic Stress Studies, San Francisco, November 1996.

Yehuda, Rachel. "Developmental Risk Factors for PTSD: Role of Parental PTSD, Childhood Trauma and Neuroendocrine Responses." Paper presented at the conference "Psychological Trauma: Maturation Processes and Therapeutic Interventions," Boston, March 23–24, 2001.

———, ed. *Risk Factors for Posttraumatic Stress Disorder*. Washington, DC: American Psychiatric Press, 1999.

Yehuda, Rachel, B. Kahlan, K. Binder-Brynes, S. Sothwick, S. Semelman, J. W. Mason, and E. L. Giller. "Low urinary cortisol excretion in Holocaust survivors with post-traumatic stress disorder. *American Journal of Psychiatry* 152 (1995): 982–86.

Yehuda, Rachel, and Alexander McFarlane. *Psychobiology of Post-Traumatic Stress Disorder*. New York: New York Academy of Sciences, 1997.

# About the Author

Patricia Romano McGraw, Ph.D., is a psychotherapist in private practice with over twenty years of experience in treating post-traumatic stress disorder and related problems. A former employee of Johns Hopkins Hospital Community Psychiatry Program, Dr. McGraw provides expert witness testimony on the subject of battered woman syndrome for court cases involving domestic violence and its effects and serves as a consultant to organizations that assist those who have suffered trauma and loss.

Dr. McGraw has had a lifelong interest in the integration of science and religion. She is a member of the Bahá'í Faith and has served as a psychologist and counselor to the Bahá'í Network on AIDS, Sexuality, Addictions, and Abuse (BNASAA) since its inception in 1989.

Dr. McGraw has eight children and step-children, five grandchildren, and a collie. She and her husband, Pete, live in the suburbs of Baltimore. She welcomes comments and questions and can be reached at www.trauma-recovery.com.

# Acknowledgments

I WANT TO BEGIN BY SAYING that this is my first book. The idea that I *could* write a book, and specifically the idea that I *should* write *this* book has come from other people.

In reality, this work is an integration of all my training and experience over more than thirty years. It is impossible to thank all of the many organizations, teachers, colleagues, clients, friends, and family who have contributed to my growth and development. Still, I would like to acknowledge a few who have played a decisive role.

I am particularly grateful to many individuals and institutions within the Bahá'í community. First I want to thank the Bahá'í Network on AIDS, Sexuality, Addictions, and Abuse (BNASAA), for whom I have been a consulting psychologist for over a decade. Years ago, one of their workshop presenters canceled his presentation at the last minute. I was spontaneously asked only hours before the presentation if I "knew anything" to present in his place. I chose the issue of trauma and the brain. Since that time, requests for repeat performances have never ceased, and with the growing interest came a demand for printed material. This book is my gift to them.

I cannot mention BNASAA without acknowledging my gratitude to the late Sam McClellan, my Bahá'í friend and mentor, who brought me into the BNASAA process and fostered my development as a therapist in various ways.

Academically oriented Bahá'í institutions also played a role in this book's development. The Wilmette Institute afforded me my first opportunity to present some of my ideas in an academic setting. Peter Murphy and Janet Richards, working within the Mid-Atlantic Region of the Association for Bahá'í Studies, planned one of their annual conferences around these topics. Their annual conferences address the practical application of spiritual principles to problems in everyday life.

I send heartfelt thanks to Terry Cassiday, my editor; Christopher Martin, her editorial assistant; and Lee Minnerly, general manager of Bahá'í Publishing. They were a delight to work with and persevered to bring this work to fruition.

Tom Tudor, a long-time friend and colleague, has run a support group for therapists treating trauma for many years. While I was a member, he and the other group members, ever devoted to innovative methods, insisted that I attend one of the first EMDR trainings in the country. Despite my own skepticism, I complied out of loyalty to the group. I can never thank them enough.

I am also grateful to my former colleagues at the Johns Hopkins Hospital Community Psychiatry Program. Their friendship and belief in my work was a great support.

I wish I could thank all of the clients with whom I have worked who were willing to share their pain and suffering with me. Since I cannot, I will thank their spokesperson, Kim, whose journal entries create the heart of this book. Despite all her suffering and repeated setbacks in life, she has remained steadfast in her determination to move forward and help others along the way.

I want to thank those who were willing to read the manuscript as it developed—in particular, Mimi Sullivan Hyde, who, early in the project, walked me through the bookstores, showed me the books, and said, "Come on, you can do this!" Her belief in the importance of the work and her honest critiques and feedback on the early chapters were absolutely invaluable.

I want to acknowledge my sons, Chris and Mike, who gave me my first joyful experience of attunement between mothers and babies. Now grown men, they are my staunch supporters and friends.

Finally, I want to thank my husband, Pete, whose ardent love has transcended both time and space. There are no words Pete, just thank you, heart to heart.

# Index

# About the Bahá'í Faith

In just over one hundred years the Bahá'í Faith has grown from an obscure movement in the Middle East to the second most widespread independent world religion after Christianity. With some 5 million adherents in virtually every corner of the globe—including people from every nation, ethnic group, culture, profession, and social or economic class—it is probably the most diverse organized body of people on the planet today.

Its founder, Bahá'u'lláh, taught that there is one God, Who progressively reveals His Will to humanity. Each of the great religions brought by the Messengers of God—Abraham and Moses, Krishna, Buddha, Zoroaster, Jesus, Muhammad, the Báb—represents a successive stage in the spiritual development of the human race. Bahá'u'lláh, the most recent Messenger in this line, has brought teachings that address the moral and spiritual challenges of today's world.

The Bahá'í Faith teaches that there is only one human race and that religion should be a source of unity; condemns all forms of prejudice and racism; upholds the equality of women and men; confirms the importance and value of marriage and the family; establishes the need for the independent investigation of the truth; insists on access to education for all; asserts the essential harmony between science and religion; declares the need to eliminate extremes of wealth and poverty; and exalts work done in a spirit of service to the level of worship.

Bahá'ís believe that religion should be a dynamic force that raises the individual, family, and community to new spiritual heights. To this end Bahá'ís all around the world work to create an atmosphere of love and unity in their own lives, in their families, and in their communities.

For more information about the Bahá'í Faith, visit
http://www.us.bahai.org/ or call 1-800-22-UNITE.

PUBLISHING

# About Bahá'í Publishing

Bahá'í Publishing produces books based on the teachings of the Bahá'í Faith, a worldwide religious community united by the belief that there is one God, one human race, and one evolving religion.

For more than a century, Bahá'í communities around the globe have been working to break down barriers of prejudice between peoples and have collaborated with other like-minded groups to promote the model of a global society. At the heart of Bahá'í teachings is the conviction that humanity is a single people with a common destiny. In the words of Bahá'u'lláh, the Founder of the Bahá'í Faith, "The earth is but one country, and mankind its citizens."

Today the Bahá'í Faith is among the fastest growing of the world religions. With some 5 million followers in virtually every country and dependent territory, it has already become the second most widespread of the world's faiths, surpassing every religion but Christianity in its geographic reach.

Bahá'í Publishing is an imprint of the Bahá'í Publishing Trust of the United States.

# Other Books Available from Bahá'í Publishing

## *The Hidden Words*

by Bahá'u'lláh

A collection of lyrical, gem-like verses of scripture that convey timeless spiritual wisdom "clothed in the garment of brevity," the Hidden Words is one of the most important and cherished scriptural works of the Bahá'í Faith.

Revealed by Bahá'u'lláh, the founder of the religion, the verses are a perfect guidebook to walking a spiritual path and drawing closer to God. They address themes such as turning to God, humility, detachment, and love, to name but a few. These verses are among Bahá'u'lláh's earliest and best known works, having been translated into more than seventy languages and read by millions worldwide. This edition will offer many American readers their first introduction to the vast collection of Bahá'í scripture.

## The Kitáb-i-Íqán:
## The Book of Certitude
by Bahá'u'lláh

The Book of Certitude is one of the most important scriptural works in all of religious history. In it Bahá'u'lláh gives a sweeping overview of religious truth, explaining the underlying unity of the world's religions, describing the universality of the revelations humankind has received from the Prophets of God, illuminating their fundamental teachings, and elucidating allegorical passages from the New Testament and the Koran that have given rise to misunderstandings among religious leaders, practitioners, and the public. Revealed in the span of two days and two nights, the work is, in the words of its translator, Shoghi Effendi, "the most important book written on the spiritual significance" of the Bahá'í Faith.

## Advancement of Women:
## A Bahá'í Perspective
by Janet A. Khan and Peter J. Khan

*Advancement of Women* presents the Bahá'í Faith's global perspective on the equality of the sexes, including:
- The meaning of equality
- The education of women and the need for their participation in the world at large
- The profound effects of equality on the family and family relationships
- The intimate relationship between equality of the sexes and global peace
- Chastity, modesty, sexual harassment, and rape

The equality of women and men is one of the basic tenets of the Bahá'í Faith, and much is said on the subject in Bahá'í writings. Until now, however, no single volume created for a general audience has provided comprehensive coverage of the Bahá'í teachings on this topic. In this broad survey, husband-and-wife team Janet and Peter Khan address even those aspects of equality of the sexes that are usually ignored or glossed over in the existing literature.

Tactfully treating a subject that often provokes argumentation, contention, polarization of attitudes, and accusations, the authors elevate the discussion to a new level that challenges all while offending none.

## The Bahá'í Faith:
## The Emerging Global Religion
### by William S. Hatcher and J. Douglas Martin

Explore the history, teachings, structure, and community life of the worldwide Bahá'í community—what may well be the most diverse organized body of people on earth—through this revised and updated comprehensive introduction (2002).

Named by the *Encylopaedia Britannica* as a book that has made "significant contributions to knowledge and understanding" of religious thought, *The Bahá'í Faith* covers the most recent developments in a Faith that, in just over 150 years, has grown to become the second most widespread of the independent world religions.

"An excellent introduction. [*The Bahá'í Faith*] offers a clear analysis of the religious and ethical values on which Bahá'ism is based (such as all-embracing peace, world harmony, the important role of women, to mention only a few)."—Annemarie Schimmel, past president, International Association for the History of Religions

"Provide[s] non-Bahá'í readers with an excellent introduction to the history, beliefs, and sociopolitical structure of a religion that originated in Persia in the mid-1800s and has since blossomed into an international organization with . . . adherents from almost every country on earth."—*Montreal Gazette*

## God Speaks Again:
## An Introduction to the Bahá'í Faith

by Kenneth E. Bowers

Written by an internationally known member of the Bahá'í community, *God Speaks Again* is the first comprehensive introduction to the Bahá'í Faith written for general readers that includes many important and beautiful passages of Bahá'í scripture to both illustrate and explain the Faith's history, teachings, and distinctive relevance for life on our planet today. The book contains 30 chapters covering all aspects of the religion, as well as notes, a glossary, a bibliography, and a suggested reading list. The history and teachings of the Bahá'í Faith center around the inspiring person of its Prophet and Founder, Bahá'u'lláh (1817–1892). The extraordinary qualities that Bahá'u'lláh displayed throughout the course of His life, the voluminous and comprehensive body of His written works, and the impact they continue to have around the globe undeniably qualify Him as a major figure in world religious history.

## Marriage beyond Black and White:
## An Interracial Family Portrait

by David Douglas and Barbara Douglas

A powerful story about the marriage of a Black man and a White woman, *Marriage beyond Black and White* offers a poignant and sometimes painful look at what it was like to be an interracial couple in the United States from the early 1940s to the mid-1990s. Breaking one of the strongest taboos in American society at the time, Barbara Wilson Tinker and Carlyle Douglas met, fell in love, married, and began raising a family. At the time of their wedding, interracial marriage was outlawed in twenty-seven states and was regarded as an anathema in the rest.

Barbara began writing their story to record both the triumphs and hardships of interracial marriage. Her son David completed the family chronicle. The result will uplift and inspire any reader whose life is touched by injustice, offering an invaluable perspective on the roles of faith and spiritual transformation in combating prejudice and racism.

## Refresh and Gladden My Spirit: Prayers and Meditations from Bahá'í Scripture
### Introduction by Pamela Brode

Discover the Bahá'í approach to prayer with this uplifting collection of prayers and short, inspirational extracts from Bahá'í scripture. More than 120 prayers in *Refresh and Gladden My Spirit* offer solace and inspiration on themes including spiritual growth, nearness to God, comfort, contentment, happiness, difficult times, healing, material needs, praise and gratitude, and strength, to name only a few. An introduction by Pamela Brode examines the powerful effects of prayer and meditation in daily life, outlines the Bahá'í approach to prayer, and considers questions such as "What is prayer?" "Why pray?" "Are our prayers answered?" and "Does prayer benefit the world?"

## Release the Sun
### by William Sears

Millennial fervor gripped many people around the world in the early nineteenth century. While Christians anticipated the return of Jesus Christ, a wave of expectation swept through Islam that the "Lord of the Age" would soon appear. In Persia, this reached a dramatic climax on May 23, 1844, when a twenty-five-year-old merchant from Shíráz named Siyyid 'Alí-Muḥammad, later titled "the Báb," announced that he was the bearer of a divine Revelation destined to transform the spiritual life of the human race. Furthermore, he claimed that he was but the herald of another Messenger, who would soon bring a far greater Revelation that would usher in an age of universal peace. Against a backdrop of wide-scale moral decay in Persian society, this declaration aroused hope and excitement among all classes. The Báb quickly attracted tens of thousands of followers, including influential members of the clergy— and the brutal hand of a fearful government bent on destroying this movement that threatened to rock the established order.

*Release the Sun* tells the extraordinary story of the Báb, the Prophet-Herald of the Bahá'í Faith. Drawing on contemporary accounts, William Sears vividly describes one of the most significant but little-known periods in religious history since the rise of Christianity and Islam.

## *Seeking Faith:*
## *Is Religion Really What You Think It Is?*
### by Nathan Rutstein

What's your concept of religion? A 2001 Gallup Poll on religion in America found that while nearly two out of three Americans claim to be a member of a church or synagogue, more than half of those polled believe that religion is losing its influence on society. *Seeking Faith* examines today's concepts of religion and the various reasons why people are searching in new directions for hope and spiritual guidance. Author Nathan Rutstein explores the need for a sense of purpose, direction, and meaning in life, and the need for spiritual solutions to global problems in the social, economic, environmental, and political realms. Rutstein also discusses the concept of the Spiritual Guide, or Divine Educator, and introduces the teachings of Bahá'u'lláh and the beliefs of the Bahá'í Faith.

## *A Wayfarer's Guide to Bringing the Sacred Home*
### by Joseph Sheppherd

What's the spiritual connection between self, family, and community? Why is it so important that we understand and cultivate these key relationships? *A Wayfarer's Guide to Bringing the Sacred Home* offers a Bahá'í perspective on issues that shape our lives and the lives of those around us: the vital role of spirituality in personal transformation, the divine nature of child-rearing and unity in the family, and the importance of overcoming barriers to building strong communities—each offering joy, hope, and confidence to a challenged world. Inspiring extracts and prayers from Bahá'í scripture are included. This is an enlightening read for anyone seeking to bring spirituality into their daily lives.

VISIT YOUR FAVORITE BOOKSTORE TODAY
TO fIND OR REQUEST THESE TITLES FROM BAHÁ'Í PUBLISHING.